which?
essential guides

WILLS AND PROBATE

DAVID BUNN

Which? Books are commissioned and published by Which? Ltd,
2 Marylebone Road, London NW1 4DF
Email: books@which.co.uk

Distributed by Littlehampton Book Services Ltd, Faraday Close, Durrington, Worthing,
West Sussex BN13 3RB

British Library Cataloguing in Publication Data
A catalogue record for this book is available from the British Library

First edition 2007
Second edition 2009

Copyright ©Which? Ltd 2007, 2009

ISBN 978 1 84490 070 1

1 3 5 7 9 10 8 6 4 2

Although the author, his employers and publishers endeavour to make sure the
information in this book is accurate and up-to-date, it is only a general guide. Before
taking action on financial, legal or medical matters you should consult a qualified
professional adviser, who can consider your individual circumstances. The author, his
employers and publishers can not accordingly accept liability for any loss or damage
suffered as a consequence of relying on the information contained in this guide.

Publisher's acknowledgements
The publishers would like to thank Jonquil Lowe and also Gavin McEwan of Turcan
Connell for advice on the law in Scotland and Tony Caher of Campbell & Caher for
advice on the law in Northern Ireland.

Edited by Emma Callery
Designed by Bob Vickers
Index by Lynda Swindells
Cover photograph by Mark Massey
Printed and bound by Charterhouse, Hatfield

Arctic Volume White is an elemental chlorine-free paper produced at Arctic Paper
Hafrestroms AB in Åsensbruk, Sweden, using timber from sustainably managed
forests. The mill is ISO14001 and EMAS certified, and has FSC certified Chain of
Custody.

For a full list of Which? Books, please call 01903 828557, access our website at
www.which.co.uk, or write to Littlehampton Book Services.
For other enquiries call 0800 252 100.

Contents

Introduction

Death comes to all of us in the end, regardless of whether we have made a will, have thought about making a will but have never got around to it, or have never let it cross our minds.

This book is intended to help at two separate stages. First, Chapters 1–5 explain why you should make a will, how to make a valid will and, by use of examples, how to give effect to your wishes. In the later section, Chapters 6–8 describe what has to be done after someone has died in order to administer his or her estate. The book also explains what happens when someone dies without having made a will. *Wills and Probate* describes the basic law and procedure in England and Wales – for those readers who live in Scotland or Northern Ireland, there are separate chapters (Chapters 9 and 10).

REASONS TO MAKE A WILL

We all know we should write a will, but it's one of those things that many of us never seem to get around to. In fact, it's estimated that 60 per cent of people die without ever having made a will.

But not writing a will can mean chaos and financial worry for your family or dependants after you've gone. Without one, you can't be sure that your money and property will be passed on according to your wishes.

If you die without a will (called dying intestate), the intestacy rules determine who inherits what. For example, if you live in England or Wales and are married or in a civil partnership with children, your partner gets only the first £250,000 of your estate plus a life interest in half the remainder. Your children will inherit the rest. Be aware that rules are different for Scotland and Northern Ireland.

Couples who aren't married or registered as a civil partnership have even more need of a will, as their partner can automatically inherit only jointly owned assets. Everything else goes to the deceased's next of kin.

You can also use your will to appoint guardians for any children under 18 (otherwise the courts will have a say in your children's future), and to prevent your heirs from having to pay too much Inheritance Tax (IHT).

THE INTRICACIES OF WILL WRITING

While most people who write their own wills or administer the estates of others are able to do so quite successfully without any deep knowledge of the law, it is as well to be aware that there are some 30 Acts of Parliament that modify the ancient, traditional rules to

An overview of the contents of this book

Making a will needn't be a long and drawn-out affair. All it requires is some thought and awareness of certain issues, all of which are described in this book. Applying for probate and administering an estate requires more time, but with care and organisation it is not an impossible feat for the layman to undertake.

Making a will

List your assets

And also consider your wishes. See pages 18-28.

Understand IHT

There are ways you can help mitigate Inheritance Tax payments. See pages 29-34.

Find out about trusts

These can be valuable additions to a will. See pages 35-6.

Draft your will

Follow the guidance to ensure all legal details are covered. See pages 38-53 and 61-74.

Online will

Advice on using online will services is on pages 13-16.

Hire a professional

Use the services of a solicitor or will writer to draw up your will. See pages 13-16.

Sign your will

Ensure you sign your will legally and in front of witnesses. See pages 59-60.

Make alterations

If you need to alter your will, there are legal ways to do this. See pages 76-82.

Store your will

Make sure your will is kept in a safe place and where others can find it. See pages 84-6.

Applying for probate

Executor or administrator

If you are an executor for a family member or friend or an administrator for an intestate family member, turn to pages 90-1 to obtain an overview of the procedure of applying for probate and then administering the estate.

provide the current body of law for making wills and administering estates and trusts. Some of the rules are very strict but others can be modified. The Wills Act 1837, the Administration of Estates Act 1925 and the Trustee Act 2000 are just three of the more important Acts. This book provides only an outline of the law of wills and probate, and cannot provide all the answers, so you may have to use other references or take advice if the issues are complicated.

It has been said that the one thing worse than not making a will is making a mess of a will. Common errors in homemade wills include not getting it properly witnessed and not clearly identifying the bequest or the person for whom it is intended. One man wrote in his will, 'All to Mother'. He was no doubt clear in his own mind where his estate was going. Unfortunately, he had always called his wife 'mother', so his will was ambiguous.

APPLYING FOR PROBATE

When it comes to applying for probate or letters of administration, the Probate Registry (district registries are to be found in most large cities) provides a special procedure for those who wish to apply without using a solicitor. This book should help such people by explaining the procedure for obtaining probate as well

The costs associated with wills and probate can vary. The figures given in this book were correct at the time it went to press.

as covering what must be done to administer the estate after probate has been granted.

This book does not try to explain all the complexities of IHT or tax-avoidance schemes (there is another *Which? Essential Guide* that does that – *Giving and Inheriting* by Jonquil Lowe), but you should be aware of the principles if you are going to make a will or administer an estate. This book should give you a good idea of what those principles are, and should give a general understanding that will enable readers to discuss more complicated tax-avoidance proposals with solicitors, accountants and financial advisers.

Many people shudder at the thought of making a will or dealing with probate, and do their best not to think of death or its consequences. However, the lack of a properly written will or even the failure of a testator to appoint sensible and competent executors can cause rifts within families that can fester for a generation or more.

The current text of an Act can be found in the statute law database at www.statutelaw.gov.uk, but take great care to follow the instructions on checking how up to date it is.

Deciding to make a will

It is never too early to make a will. Anybody over the age of 18 can do one. Indeed, it is a sensible precaution because you will then know where your estate will be going on your death and who will be dealing with it. This section discusses why you should make a will and how.

Why you should make a will

For most people, what happens to their property and family when they die is a matter of importance, but others fear making a will as if to do so would somehow tempt providence. More commonly, people die without having made a will because they have just not got around to it.

Here are some very good reasons as to why you should make a will:

- You can put your affairs in order and leave clear instructions to provide for your spouse or civil partner and family.
- You can choose who should be your executors.
- You can make proper financial arrangements for your children if they are under 18 at the date of your death, as well as appointing a guardian to look after them.
- To reduce or eliminate Inheritance Tax (IHT). Properly made wills can frequently save tens of thousands of pounds in IHT.
- To make special provisions for children who may have health, matrimonial or financial problems, thereby ensuring that the wrong people do not get their hands on your money.
- To minimise the effect of long-term nursing care on the family fortunes.

- To set out what sort of funeral you would like.
- To avoid disputes within the family.

Equally, there are significant things that may happen if you don't make a will:

- IHT. If you and your spouse, or civil partner have a sizeable estate, your beneficiaries could end up paying IHT, which could have been reduced or avoided with a carefully written will.
- If you re-marry, the children of your first marriage may not get anything on your death.
- Your spouse or civil partner may not be adequately provided for.
- If you have a partner to whom you are not married, he or she will receive nothing on your death and, although your partner may be able to make a claim against your estate, their opponents may be your (and their) infant children. The costs of such an application will reduce the estate.
- The intestacy provisions may give part or all of your estate to someone you would not want to benefit and may not provide for someone dear to you.

❝ By writing your will you can put your affairs in order and leave instructions for your family. ❞

DYING INTESTATE

If you die without having made a will, you will be said to have died intestate, which means that intestacy rules then apply. If that happens, the administration of your affairs after death will be by your closest surviving next of kin in the following order:

- The deceased's spouse or civil partner.
- The children of the deceased or their **issue** (if over 18) if a child of the deceased has died before the deceased.
- The parents of the deceased.
- The brothers and sisters of the whole blood or their issue, if any of the brothers and sisters have died before the deceased.
- The brothers or sisters of the half-blood or their issue (as above).
- The grandparents.
- The uncles and aunts of the whole blood or their issue (as above).
- The uncles or aunts of the half-blood or their issue (as above).

Jargon buster

Issue Your children and all subsequent generations arising from them, that is, grandchildren, great-grandchildren, and so on.

Until 1970, the only blood relationships that the rules governing intestacy recognised were legitimate ones; an illegitimate person could not claim any interest. Now, no distinction is made between legitimate, adopted or illegitimate relationships. They are all treated equally. Normally, a court order would be required to prove a link between an illegitimate child and its father if the father was not a signatory to the birth certificate. However, the advances in blood and DNA analysis have made such proof easy to obtain. It is in the fields of artificial insemination by donor, embryo donation and surrogate motherhood where the issues become complicated, not forgetting the distinction between brothers and sisters of the whole blood and brothers and sisters of the half-blood.

❝ If you don't make a will, you die 'intestate'. ❞

An adopted child is deemed to be the legal child of his or her adoptive parents and has exactly the same inheritance rights as the adoptive parents' other (natural) children, but adoption removes any rights he or she may have had in law to his or her natural parents' estate. Similarly, the natural parents of an

For more information on what happens if you die without leaving a will, see 'Entitlement on intestacy' on pages 143–4.

adopted child lose their right to claim against the estate of that child under intestacy laws. (However, a natural parent can, of course, still benefit such a child in his or her will and vice versa.)

When it comes to disposing of your estate, your beneficiaries will also be determined by the same order of surviving next of kin. In addition, there are strict rules as to how your estate is divided. Here are some examples of what might happen if you die intestate (for complete details see pages 143–4):

- **If there is a surviving spouse or civil partner and children,** the surviving spouse or partner only gets the first £250,000 of the estate (which may mean that he or she does not even inherit the matrimonial home absolutely) and the interest in half the remainder for life. The children of the deceased get half the remainder immediately and the other half on their second parent's death.
- **If there is no spouse, civil partner or children,** the estate is divided between blood relatives in the particular order outlined on page 11.
- **If you are not married to your partner,** he or she gets nothing on your death, however long you have been together and however many children you have with them.
- **If you do not have any close relatives,** it can be difficult and expensive to trace all those entitled to share in your estate. It could even go to the crown.

Civil partnerships

The law applies to civil partners as it applies to spouses; so references to such subjects as 'husband', 'wife', 'marriage' and 'divorce' in this book should be read as referring to civil partners as well.

If you make a will, you can decide who should administer your estate and who should (and should not) benefit from it. You may also be able to ensure that no unnecessary IHT is paid on your estate.

❝When someone dies intestate, there are strict rules as to how the estate is divided up, determined by the order of surviving next of kin.❞

Using professional services

It is best practice to use an appropriate professional to write your will. It is possible to write your own, but the potential legal implications are such that it's best not to embark on this journey unless you are aware of the pitfalls.

USING A SOLICITOR

If you choose to use a solicitor to prepare your will, you will have to pay for that service (see pages 14–15). If you have not used a solicitor before, you will be pleased to know that:

- **They are obliged by law** to provide you with certain information about the job you have asked them to do.
- **They must give you the best information** they can about the cost of the work and the time it is likely to take if this is a factor in the calculation of their fee.
- **They must make clear** what work they will be doing for you.
- **They must operate** a complaint handling procedure.

DOING IT ONLINE

Many online will-writing services have developed recently (see in this chapter and pages 73–4). Which? has one such service at www.whichwills.com. The result is that there is now little justification for taking the DIY route and writing your own will. The price of doing it online is very reasonable and should not exclude anyone with straightforward circumstances. In this book you will find information to help you decide if you are

---

Finding an online service

When looking for an online service consider:

- **Is it a reputable provider?**
- **Does it provide a telephone advice service?**
- **Does it ask questions to see that your circumstances are suitable for the service?**
- **Does it offer a solicitor to check the will?**
- **Can you leave the service and return to it after some time has elapsed?**

If you want to write your own will, some salient points are outlined on pages 73-4, but it is important that you judge your abilities realisitically - see page 14. The website for the Which? Wills service is www.whichwills.com.

a suitable candidate to use an online will service.

The advantages of using one are cost and convenience. The disadvantages are that you will not get the personal ongoing reassurance of a solicitor that you are making a will that is appropriate for your circumstances and that there are no complications or other factors that you should be considering. However, quality online will services offer telephone advice from a solicitor throughout the entire process to ensure that all your questions and concerns are answered.

USING A WILL WRITER

There are various companies and individuals who advertise will-writing services. These offers can look attractive because the cost is usually (but not always) less than what a solicitor would charge (see pages 14–15). Some state that the preparation of the will is supervised by solicitors.

Don't assume that a will-writing service will also sort out your tax planning for you. It is hard to generalise about the quality of service you will get from these companies but, if you decide to use one, you should check the qualification of the person who is to prepare your will and what comeback your executors would have if they found the will to be defective after your death, some 20 years later. If you decide to use

You may find that a number of solicitors (and will-writing firms) offer an internet service. However, a quality online service will have a solicitor on hand to answer any queries – just in case you misunderstand what you read on a website.

a will-writing company, make sure that it belongs to the Society of Will Writers or the Institute of Professional Willwriters (see box, below). Ask for evidence of indemnity insurance, too.

It is hard to see why you should use a will writer. If your circumstances are straightforward and you do not want to pay for advice, an online service should meet your needs. If your circumstances are not straightforward or you do feel you need advice, a solicitor may be more appropriate. One of the big organisations for will writers advises against online services; the other seems to be connected to one.

WRITING YOUR WILL YOURSELF

It is possible to write your own will and many people do so successfully, but it is

To contact the Society of Will Writers, go to www.thesocietyofwillwriters.co.uk; for the Institute of Professional Willwriters, go to: www.jpw.org.uk.

also very easy to make a mistake when writing the will or signing it, which can render it invalid or ambiguous. For advice on writing your own, see pages 73–4.

WHAT IT MIGHT COST

To ask a solicitor 'What will it cost to make a will?' is rather like asking a car salesman 'What will it cost to buy a car?' The cost of a will is determined by a number of factors:

- **The time** the solicitor spends discussing your circumstances and wishes and explaining the consequences of those wishes (this can easily exceed an hour).
- **The situation and size** of the solicitor's firm (large firms in city centres are generally more expensive than small firms in less expensive locations).
- **The seniority/experience** of the solicitor (the more experienced the solicitor, the higher his hourly charging rate).
- **The time it takes to draft the will.**

If your circumstances are straightforward and the provisions of your will are simple, the cost may not exceed £250 plus VAT. But if the initial interview exceeds an hour (there may be more than one interview), and that is followed by some complicated drafting to create a discretionary trust (see pages 35–6) after discussions with an accountant and financial adviser, then you must expect the cost of the will to fall somewhere between £400 and £750, or even more. If an identical will is

---

Using the Legal Help scheme

If your disposable income is below a certain level, or you receive income support or family credit and your savings are within certain limits, you will be entitled to receive free legal advice under a scheme called Legal Help (for contacts, see box, below). Unfortunately, Legal Help does not cover the making of wills unless, as well as being eligible under the scheme, you fall into one of the following categories:

- You are over 70 years old.
- You are seriously disabled or visually or hearing impaired.
- You are the parent of a child who fits into the above category.
- You are a single parent wanting to appoint a guardian for your child.

Legal Help allows people with a low income to get free legal advice and help from a solicitor or an experienced legal adviser. For more information, go to the Citizens Advice Bureau website at www.citizensadvice.org.uk.

prepared for your spouse or civil partner at the same time, you should expect to get a good discount on the second will.

All that may drive you to consider writing your own will, but, before you do, remember that the solicitor who is advising you is covered by indemnity insurance should his or her advice turn out to be negligent. If the advice is good, it could save your estate from paying unnecessary IHT. For those who do not have the knowledge and courage to prepare their own wills, the cost of having it done for you is likely to be money well spent. An online will-writing service, such as that provided by Which?, may be a good middle way.

CHOOSING A SOLICITOR

A recommendation from a friend who has used a solicitor to prepare a will or deal with a probate matter is a good start. If no such information is available, the Law Society website (see box, below) should list local solicitors, their firms and the legal topics in which they specialise.

Having found a solicitor, the next step is to ask what information he or she will need to advise you and for your solicitor to send you the firm's terms of business for preparing your will. You may find that some solicitors are prepared to give a fixed price at the outset once they know what you want, but others may only be willing to give you an estimate of the

time your will should take together with their hourly rate. In those circumstances, you can ask for a ceiling price.

When you approach a solicitor to make your will, you may be given a checklist and set of notes to help you get the important information together. This will include details of your assets, your spouse or civil partner's assets, property values, investment valuations, pension fund valuations and your debts (see pages 18–19). It would also be sensible to familiarise yourself with the basics of IHT (see pages 29–34).

Once you have had an in-depth meeting with your solicitor, you should expect to receive a draft will within two weeks and then the final version should be ready to sign within a week or so of approving the solicitor's draft. However, not all solicitors are as fast as that, so ask for a time estimate.

 Signing the will is an important act. If you do not sign yours with your solicitor as one of your witnesses, make sure you comply with the legal requirements (see pages 59-60). Wills are often invalidated by incorrect signing procedures.

 For more advice and information on choosing a solicitor, contact the Law Society of England and Wales on www.lawsociety.org.uk.

Factors to consider

This chapter covers preliminary issues to do with
making a will, starting with establishing what your
assets are and then considering your circumstances.
Inheritance Tax and trusts are also important
subjects to understand before you start drafting
your will – they are covered on pages 29-36.

Your assets and wishes

The way to avoid ambiguity is to be very clear in the language you use in your will. As a first step, be clear in your own mind about your assets and your wishes.

YOUR ASSETS

Start by drawing up a list of your assets, which are anything you own, such as cash, investments, a house and other personal possessions. You may not feel wealthy, but you are probably worth more than you realise. Property prices have risen over the years, so if you own a house, it is probably worth quite a bit. To help you work out your assets, a checklist is provided opposite. If the value of your assets exceeds £325,000, or if you are married or in a civil partnership £650,000 (2009–10) when added to your partner's assets, there could be IHT to pay (see pages 29–34).

❝ You may not feel wealthy, but it can be surprising just how quickly your assets add up to a substantial amount of money. ❞

YOUR WISHES

People often have conflicting wishes, which have to be resolved or compromised before making a will. Is the purpose of your will to:

- Reduce your potential tax bill as much as possible?
- Provide for your spouse or civil partner?
- Help your children get established?
- Provide for a charity of your choice?
- Provide for the children of your first marriage as well as your present spouse or civil partner?
- Provide for your cohabitee who otherwise would get nothing?

You will have to decide where you stand on these issues before making your will.

 It would be very considerate to your executors if you were to regularly update this asset checklist. See pages 106–22 for the type of information that your executors will need in order to apply for probate.

Asset checklist

Fill in the boxes below, even if it is only an approximate value. You need not be too exact about this, because it is bound to change by the time you die. The assets you have at the present time will change in value – you will acquire new ones and dispose of some of those that you have.

1 Property

Your home	£
Your second or holiday home/caravan	£
Your household contents (furniture, clothes, etc.)	£
Antiques	£
Jewellery	£
Your car	£
Other items of value	£
SUB-TOTAL:	

2 Financial

Bank accounts	£
Building Society account	£
Stocks and shares	£
National Savings	£
Pension/benefits	£
Life assurance	£
Premium Bonds	£
Unit trusts	£
Business assets	£
Any other financial interests	£
SUB-TOTAL:	

3 Money you are owed

Debtor's name:

Debtor's address:

Date of loan:

Amount outstanding	£
SUB-TOTAL:	

4 Money you owe

(unless these will be paid off on your death, for example, by an insurance policy)

Mortgage outstanding	£
Other loans	£
Overdraft	£
Hire purchase	£
Credit card debts	£
Other money owed	£
SUB-TOTAL:	

To establish the approximate size of your estate, add together the sub-totals in groups 1, 2 and 3 and subtract the answer from group 4.

TOTAL VALUE OF ESTATE:

Your circumstances

When you are considering writing a will, there are certain circumstances that you should be aware of so that you can discuss your potential options with your solicitor or will writer.

YOUR ASSETS EXCEED £300,000

The threshold at which you will incur Inheritance Tax (IHT) is £325,000 in the tax year 2009–10 (see the chart below for the projected IHT limits published by the government up until 2010). Keeping down IHT is an important planning area when a will is being written, so if your assets exceed the limit, be aware there are things that can be done to help reduce the potential tax bill – see pages 29–34.

IHT-free limit

Tax year	Tax-free limit
2009-10	£325,000
2010-11	£350,000

❝ If you are married or civil partners, your nil-rate bands are now treated as one allowance of £650,000, but you still need to make a will to avoid intestacy. ❞

YOU ARE MARRIED

The Finance Act 2008 raised the threshold for IHT to £650,000 for married couples and civil partners (for intestacy rules, see page 143). Couples who are married or in a civil partnership can now merge their two £325,000 allowances to make one larger one, removing the need to make provision in a will to make use of both nil-rate bands. The new allowance applies to widows and widowers who can make backdated claims (see pages 29–34).

Traditionally, a husband (or wife) would give the main part of the estate to his wife (or her husband) so that the surviving partner becomes the **residuary beneficiary**. On the first death, the survivor would, if necessary, make a fresh will, providing for his or her chosen beneficiaries (usually the children).

Both partners might be victims of the same road accident, one being killed outright and the other surviving for a few days but then dying without making a new will. In this case, the couple's intention of leaving everything to the survivor would have been defeated. When this happens and the will makes no alternative provisions, the property that is inherited by the 'short-term' survivor is distributed according to the rules of intestacy (see page 11) (although there are special rules that apply when married partners die intestate and it is not known who died first). To overcome the potential problem that the intestacy rules might well not accord with the deceased's wishes, a specific provision for this possibility should be made in the will. It should be stated who the property should go to in the event of the partner not surviving the **testator**. In many cases, this would be the children.

To cover the case of such a joint accident in which it is impossible to know who will survive whom and by how long, a will can contain a provision that the wife, husband or civil partner will inherit the property provided that person survives for a given number of days and, if that does not happen, that the property goes to a **named person** or **class of persons** or 'another beneficiary'. This is known as a survivorship clause, but you must be careful of the IHT consequences if you include such a clause in your will (see pages 56–7).

❝ The most usual beneficiaries in wills are partners and children. ❞

YOU ARE AN UNMARRIED COUPLE

The intestacy rules that apply to married or civil partners do not apply to an unmarried couple, even if they have lived together for ten years, have six children and call themselves Mr and Mrs Smith. In such a case, when an unmarried parent dies, the whole of the estate is divided between the children of that parent because there is no surviving spouse or civil partner. If there are no children, the estate passes to the parents of the deceased, and if there are no living parents, the siblings of the deceased will benefit. It is therefore essential for cohabiting couples to make wills to provide for one another.

YOU HAVE CHILDREN

If you have children, you must watch out for the following when making your will:

- **If you leave property to your children without being specific,** you are, by default, including any illegitimate children you may have, children of a previous marriage and any adopted children (who do not have the right to inherit from their natural parents). Stepchildren are not included unless they are specifically mentioned.
- A child will receive his or her benefit at the age of 18 unless the will requires

Trusts are an important part of inheritance planning and will writing. For more information on the subjects, see pages 35-6.

21

him or her to be older – say 21. If the child is under 18 when you die, it is the job of the executors to look after the money for him or her until he or she reaches the age at which the money can be paid. However, this rule is modified by the provisions of the Trustee Act 1925, which allows a proportion of the gift to be applied by the trustees, before the child is 18, for his or her maintenance, education or benefit.

If you are concerned that a beneficiary may not be ready for such financial responsibility, even though he or she is 18 years old, you can create a trust according to which the trustees can be instructed to delay payment until the beneficiary shows signs of financial wisdom. If the problems are more intractable (if your child is a drug addict, say), you may wish to consider creating a trust that can provide accommodation and medical treatment for the beneficiary without giving him or her access to large sums of money.

Likewise, if the beneficiary is insolvent and on the road to bankruptcy, it would be sensible to create a trust such that the trustees can wait and see before making any payment to the beneficiary. A discretionary trust would provide such flexibility (see pages 35–6).

To prevent the possible circumstances occurring as described in 'You have children and have remarried' (see page 26), you could leave each other a **life interest** in part of your capital assets, ensuring that, on the death of the survivor, the assets pass to the children. Alternatively, you could make a will containing a discretionary trust (see page 35) in which the surviving partner and children would be potential beneficiaries. In that case, a letter of wishes could be placed with the will explaining to the trustees how you would like the assets eventually to be passed on to the children. A letter of wishes is not legally binding, but conveys your wihes to your trustees.

Jargon buster

Class of persons A group of people with a particular common link, e.g. all my grandchildren, or all my first cousins

Domicile The country you consider to be your permanent home even if you actually reside elsewhere. It is distinct from nationality and place of residence

Life interest A gift that gives someone the right to income from an asset or the right to occupation of a property for the duration of their life, after which the asset or property passes to someone else mentioned in the gift (known as the remainder man)

Named person A person who is named in the will

Residuary beneficiary A person who gets or shares what is left of the estate after all debts, taxes and specific legacies have been paid

Testator A person who makes a will

YOU HAVE JOINTLY OWNED PROPERTY AND ASSETS

Joint ownership of a house can be set up in one of two ways.

- 'Joint tenancy' means that on the death of one joint owner the deceased person's share passes automatically to the survivor. This is the usual arrangement for married couples and civil partnerships, but be aware that it bypasses anything you might say in your will about your share of the house.
- A 'tenancy in common' means that, on the death of one joint owner, the deceased person's share passes according to his or her will. If the will does not limit the circumstances under which the property can be sold, the person who inherits the half-share can compel the owner of the other half-share to join in a sale of the property so they can both realise their asset.

These arrangements do not alter IHT liability, which may be charged on a half-share passing to the surviving joint tenant – unless the estate, including the value of the half-share, is under the nil-rate band or the half-share is exempt because it is passing to the surviving spouse or civil partner.

IHT planning for married couples or civil partners who are joint owners of a house is now more straightforward thanks to recent legislation in October 2007. There is now no need for couples to make provision in their wills to ensure they make the most of both their nil-rate bands as they can automatically merge their £325,000 allowances into one £650,000 allowance.

The intestacy rules have changed for deaths after 1 February 2009. If a spouse or civil partner dies with assets of £325,000 but no will, the survivor (with children) will only get capital of £250,000 (see page 143).

YOU OWN A FOREIGN PROPERTY OR DO NOT HAVE BRITISH DOMICILE

It is now quite common for British nationals to own property abroad. If you do own foreign property or have non-British domicile, you must establish what happens to the property on your death under the laws of the country in which the property is located. In some cases, your spouse and children get a fixed share, whatever your will says (but probably not your civil partner). Generally speaking, you should have a will prepared by a local lawyer to dispose of the property on your death, but remember

---

! If you wish to 'sever the joint tenancy' in order to create a tenancy in common, write a notice to the other joint tenant giving him or her notice that you are severing the joint tenancy. You must also notify the Land Registry on form RX1: see www.landregistry.gov.uk/assets/library/documents/rx1.pdf.

to modify any clause in your UK will that revokes earlier wills (see page 56).

Your domicile is also an issue if it is not in England, Wales, Scotland or Northern Ireland, as the law of your country of domicile may overrule some or all of the provisions of your British will. If you have made your will abroad, you should take local advice.

If there is any foreign element in your affairs, you should not use an online service or write your own will. You have a foreign element if you have property abroad or are of foreign origin (such as if your parents lived abroad permanently when you were born) or are married to such a person. Your domicile refers to the territory of your permanent home; this is a simplification because the law on this is obscure and you should take advice if there are any foreign circumstances in your origin or life. For example, a person may originate in California but leave there and never intend to return. But if she settles with a Frenchman living in the UK and in Malta, it may be very difficult to say where her permanent home is (and the law may say it is still California).

YOU HAVE DEBTS, MORTGAGES AND CONNECTED LIFE POLICIES

Debts do not disappear when you die. An exception to this rule occurs when your debts are greater than your assets – what happens then is that the assets you have will be shared among your creditors (after your funeral expenses have been deducted) and your estate will be declared insolvent. Where the assets are greater than the liabilities, your estate will have to meet all these liabilities before anything can be paid to the beneficiaries (see pages 121–2).

Look closely at any mortgage debt. If you are leaving a mortgaged house to a beneficiary, that person will become responsible for paying off the mortgage unless your will sets out a contrary intention. Matters can be made worse if there is an insurance policy that you are assuming will be used to pay off the mortgage. Unless the policy or the will makes your intention clear, you may find that the insurance money ends up in the residue of your estate going to one person while the house, subject to a mortgage, goes to another.

Most debts will be notified to, and paid by, your executors from the assets of your estate, but the situation can be much more complicated if you are paying maintenance to an ex-spouse or ex-civil partner under a court order. In such cases, the 'ex' will be able to make a claim against your estate unless a reasonable provision for that person is made in your will (see divorce, opposite).

 To find a local lawyer in the country where you own property, contact the Law Society. The website addresses are www.lawsociety.org.uk (England and Wales), www.lawsoc-ni.org (Northern Ireland), wwww.lawscot.org.uk (Scotland) and www.lawsociety.ie (Ireland).

YOU ARE DIVORCED OR GOING THROUGH DIVORCE

If you are going through a divorce, you may be comforted by the thought that the issue of the decree absolute automatically deletes from your will any benefit directed to your ex-spouse or ex-civil partner. Unfortunately, that may not be the end of the story. If you have agreed to pay maintenance to your ex-partner, or if the financial settlement is not finally resolved at your death, your ex-partner may decide to issue proceedings under the Inheritance (Provision for Family and Dependants) Act 1975 in order to claim some or all of your estate (see page 53).

If you wish to make a gift by your will to a person who is involved in divorce proceedings, you may find that your gift is claimed as a financial resource by the opposing spouse or civil partner. In such cases, the creation of a discretionary trust (see page 35) may protect your estate from such claims. Alternatively, you might decide to make your gift to the children of the divorcing beneficiary.

YOU HAVE A CHILD WHO MAY DIVORCE

In the event of parents being concerned that the marriage of one of their children will end in divorce and they wish to prevent the other spouse or civil partner from benefiting from their estate, the best course of action would be to set up a discretionary trust (see pages 35–6). In this instance, the child would be named as the potential beneficiary

and the wish would be expressed to carefully chosen trustees that the state of the child's marriage be noted before any payments were made to him or her.

YOU LIVE ON YOUR OWN AND HAVE CHILDREN

If your children are under 18, it would be irresponsible not to make a will. The will should appoint guardians to care for the children even if the missing parent is alive and has parental responsiblity as that person may die before you or be an unsuitable parent for some reason. You should also consider how a guardian might be reimbursed so that he or she does not suffer financial loss by looking after your children. In addition, you can decide who your executors/trustees should be as they will be responsible for looking after your estate until your children become adults (you might even consider including a discretionary trust in your will, which would enable your trustees to delay payment to a child who was a drug addict or tangled up with matrimonial or financial problems – see pages 35–6).

YOU HAVE CHILDREN AND ARE PLANNING TO REMARRY

In this instance, it is essential that you discuss the subject of wills with your spouse- or civil partner-to-be. If he or she already has children, he or she will have the same concerns as you.

If you want your estate eventually to go to the children of your first marriage, look carefully at the financial consequences if you die shortly after your

25

Mr Johnson dies, leaving Mrs Johnson and 25-year-old twins called Robert and William. Mrs Johnson then marries Mr Forbes two years later, but forgets to make a new will. Mrs Forbes is then killed in a car accident, leaving an estate of £120,000, which passes on her intestacy to Mr Forbes. Mr Forbes eventually gets over his grief and marries his doctor, Liz Adams, but dies of a heart attack on his honeymoon.

Mr Forbes has made a will in consideration of marriage to and in favour of his wife to the exclusion of his two stepsons. The result is not what Mr or Mrs Johnson would have expected or wanted.

remarriage (see 'You have children and have remarried, right). A common decision is for one spouse or civil partner to sell his or her present house and to purchase a half-share in the other's house. Do this as tenants in common (see page 23) so that the wills can provide for the survivor to live there for life, or for a specific period after which the children of the deceased spouse or civil partner could recover their parent's share in the house.

Where one party has children and the other does not, the final decision will depend upon the wealth of the parties, the length of time they have been together and the strength (or otherwise) of the relationship between the surviving spouse or civil partner and the stepchildren. The important thing is to bring this issue into the open before the second marriage so you both know what the deal is to be, and then put it all in writing.

YOU HAVE CHILDREN AND HAVE REMARRIED

In this instance, it's important to make a new will to protect the interests of your children in the event of your death, if you haven't done so already (see the case study, above).

YOU, YOUR SPOUSE OR CIVIL PARTNER IS IN A HOME

If one spouse or civil partner has to go into a residential or nursing home, the fit spouse or civil partner can leave his or her assets (including his or her share of the house), to any child rather than leaving it to the sick or elderly spouse

❝A gift of capital or income to someone being cared for in a residential home and in receipt of means-tested benefits, might result in those benefits being withdrawn.❞

or partner so it would reduce the means-tested benefits received by the spouse who is resident in a home.

If you are already in a home, it is not too late to make a will but, unless your fees are being paid from income, it is unlikely that your assets will survive more than a few years of nursing home fees. If you have significant assets that you hope to leave to your family, you should be considering IHT mitigation, which can take assets out of the estate of a testator, thus removing them from the claims of others, such as the Benefits Agency. If you are concerned about the cost of nursing care and its effect on your estate, you should take professional advice to establish if there are any anti-avoidance measures and what you could do about them.

YOU RUN A BUSINESS OR FARM

Businesses and farms can be run as private companies, partnerships or by a sole proprietor. In all cases, special IHT rules apply, which give tax relief. The IHT relief can be 100 per cent, and even when the relief is less, there may still be concessions that allow the tax to be paid by instalments.

If you wish to bequeath shares in a private company, it would be sensible to establish how they would be valued on your death. If you have a controlling interest in the company, the Capital Taxes Office at HM Revenue & Customs (www.hmrc.gov.uk/inheritancetax) will look at the value of the controlling interest, not just the value of the shares. You should also find out whether the

shares can be left to anyone you wish or whether they have to be offered for sale to existing shareholders first.

Where the business or farm is run as a partnership, it is important to understand what the partnership agreement says in the event of the death of a partner. It may give the surviving partner the right to buy the deceased partner's share, but it may also set down other arrangements, which would have to be observed by the executors of the deceased partner. In exceptional cases, it may even give the deceased partner the right by will to introduce another partner as his or her successor. If there is no written partnership agreement, the matter will be determined under the provisions of the Partnership Act 1890.

If you are in a partnership, look carefully at the arrangements in place should one of you die. If the surviving partner hopes to carry on the business, it would be sensible to agree terms now and to consider insuring each other's lives in order to pay out the claims of a deceased partner's spouse or children.

Jargon buster

Legacy A gift of money or object
Residue The amount left in an estate after all expenses, such as the funeral and outstanding IHT debts and legacies, have been paid

YOU INTEND TO LEAVE MONEY TO A CHARITY

If you are intending to leave money to a charity, make sure it still exists as a registered charity and that you have the correct name and address in your will. Some charities have quite similar names so confusion could easily occur. To avoid this confusion, quote their charitable registration number.

If you are intending to leave something quite substantial, such as a house, check with the charity first because it may be able to suggest a suitable clause.

One benefit that is common to all charitable gifts is that they are free of IHT (assuming your estate exceeds the nil-rate band), but the way in which an estate is divided between an ordinary beneficiary and a charity can increase or decrease the amount received by the charity. If the individual gets a **legacy** to bear its own tax and the charity gets the **residue**, the residue can be greater than if the charity got the legacy and the individual got the residue, subject to IHT.

For example, if your estate is worth £435,000 and you make a gift of £60,000 to a charity, the balance remaining is £375,000. Out of this, £20,000 has to be paid in IHT, so the individual gets £355,000 (IHT is calculated by subtracting the charitable bequest from the estate to leave £375,000 and then subtracting the nil-rate band of £325,000 to give £50,000 on which tax is £20,000, at 40 per cent).

If, however, you make a specific gift of £360,000 to an individual (the gift to bear its own tax) and then give the residue to the charity, the individual will get £346,000, the tax will be £14,000 and so the charity gets £75,000. The £9,000 reduction in what the individual will get has resulted in a £25,000 increase in what the charity will get.

YOU HAVE A PET

If you have a dog or some other pet that might outlive you, it would be sensible to think what you would want to happen to it in the event of your death. You should be realistic about your wishes and what it will cost to carry them out. If you own cattle or horses, you should have a contingency plan known to others before your death.

YOU HAVE OTHER SPECIAL BEQUESTS

If you wish to leave something to person who is being cared for in a residential home and who is in receipt of means-tested benefits, be aware that a gift of capital or income to such a person could result in those benefits being withdrawn. The creation of a discretionary trust (see page 35) in which the beneficiary has no absolute right to benefit may be the best solution for this problem, but it is wise to take advice in such circumstances.

Inheritance Tax

Inheritance Tax (IHT) is the only form of tax or duty imposed on the death of a person whose domicile is in the UK. For many years the tax was known as estate duty. In 1975, this was changed to capital transfer tax to reflect the fact that it affected not only the property that passed from one person to another on the former's death, but was also a tax on the larger gifts that people made in their own lifetimes.

IHT is charged at 40 per cent and is liable to be paid on the value of an estate (including certain gifts and trust assets) that is more than £325,000, or £650,000 for married couples and civil partners (2009–10). Estates that are valued at less than £325,000 are in the 'nil-rate band'.

One of the reasons for making a will is to reduce the IHT that might be charged on your death or, later, on the death of your spouse or civil partner. It is important that you understand the tax well enough to know if you are going to be affected by it.

This book also suggests a number of ways to potentially reduce the incidence of IHT so that you can discuss the matter thoroughly with your solicitor or your independent financial adviser if you decide not to tackle the job yourself.

WHEN IS IHT PAYABLE?

On a person's death, IHT is charged on the value of his or her net estate in excess of the nil-rate band – that is, all his or her property and assets less all his or her liabilities and debts (see page 19). (The funeral costs can also be deducted.)

The Inheritance Tax Act 1984 (originally known as the Capital Transfer Tax Act 1984) states that IHT 'shall be charged on the value transferred by a chargeable transfer'. To prevent people giving away all their property immediately before they die in a bid to avoid the tax, the rules provide that IHT is calculated not only on the value of the property that a deceased person has when he or she dies but also on the running total of gifts ('transfers') over the last seven years. So, when calculating the size of an estate, it is important to look at all the gifts made

If you have a complex or very large estate, get professional advice on ways to minimise paying IHT. Contact either a solicitor or a member of the Society of Trust and Estate Practioners (STEP) (see page 41).

in the seven years up to and including the gift on death. The tax is applied first to these gifts and then to the estate. The effect is often to use up the nil-rate band on the gifts so the tax payable on the estate is increased (see the example on page 32). IHT relates mainly to property passing on death but also affects lifetime gifts, unless they fall into an exempt category (see tax-free gifts, right).

The value on which IHT is charged also includes the capital value of any **trust** set up before 22 March 2006 in which the deceased had a **life interest** or was entitled to the income or was entitled to the use of property, such as a home. (Most life interest trusts set up on or after that date do not count as part of

the estate because they will have been subject to tax instead during the deceased's lifetime.)

The amount of any taxable gifts made by the deceased up to seven years prior to the death or even earlier gifts if an interest or benefit has been reserved is also added back to give the total value upon which IHT will be levied.

TAX-FREE GIFTS

The following gifts do not need to be taken into consideration when calculating what needs to be added to an estate from gifts given over the last seven years of a deceased's life. As such, they are useful to know about for will planning.

- **£3,000 per annum,** all or part of which can be carried forward for one year if unused (every individual has this allowance). Gifts always use up this year's allowance first before any carried forward part.
- **Small present**s – any number of individual gifts of up to £250 per recipient can be made each year in addition to the annual allowance of £3,000. Note that the same person cannot receive £3,000 as well as £250 under these provisions.
- **Gifts to a spouse or civil partner** – all property passing between husband and wife or between civil partners. Any property that passes from one spouse

Giving and Inheriting, a *Which? Essential Guide* is another invaluable source of information on the topic of Inheritance Tax.

to another by gift in their lifetime, or to the survivor on the first death is wholly exempt from IHT. This provision does not apply to unmarried couples or unregistered same-sex couples.

- **Gifts to a person in consideration of their marriage,** up to £5,000 per parent, £2,500 per grandparent and £1,000 from anyone else.
- **Normal expenditure out of income** – what is normal expenditure depends on the income and spending habits of the giver, but this can be a valuable exemption.
- **Charities** – all gifts, regardless of size, by will to charity are wholly exempt from IHT.
- **Political parties** – gifts in lifetime or by a will to established political parties are exempt. The condition is that the party has at least 2 MPs or polled at least 150,000 votes at the most recent general election, so it need not be to one of the main parties.
- **Gifts in lifetime or on death to the nation** or of public benefit – gifts to certain national museums or collections and some objects or property of national importance are exempt if they are accepted.
- **Gifts in lifetime or on death to housing associations.**
- **Gifts in lifetime for maintenance of family.** (These are subject to detailed provisions as laid down in the Inheritance Act 1984.)
- **Transfer of pools and lottery wins** according to an agreement made before the win.

There are also a number of variable exemptions or 'reliefs' affecting such types of property as Lloyd's underwriting accounts, farmland, forestry and timber, sole trader and partnership businesses and family company shares. You should get advice from a solicitor or accountant if you are involved with any of these. The qualification rules for these reliefs are complicated and so is the calculation of the figures involved, so seek further guidance from an expert.

POTENTIALLY EXEMPT TRANSFERS (PETS)

In addition to the tax-free gifts listed above, you are permitted to give lifetime gifts to individuals that remain tax-free – as long as you survive for seven years after giving them. But PETs given over the last seven years of your life are included in the value of your estate when assessing any IHT liability. The gifts are treated as

Insuring against a PET

A beneficiary of a lifetime gift in excess of the nil-rate band might want to consider taking out a form of term life insurance payable to the beneficiary so that, if the donor dies within the seven-year period, the policy will provide an amount equal to the tax that would become payable. This is only relevant where the lifetime gifts of the donor exceed the nil-rate band, taking into account the running total of gifts over seven years.

the first slice of the estate for calculating IHT. For example, a gift of a house worth £400,000 two years before death with an estate of £100,000 results in tax of £30,000 on the gift and £40,000 on the estate. The total IHT payable is the same as for an estate of £500,000 with no gifts, but the tax is distributed between the estate and the recipient of the gift. If the gift had been £100,000 and the estate worth £400,000, the recipient would pay nothing because the gift, as the first slice of value charged to the tax, would fall in the nil-rate band. Only £225,000 of the nil-rate band would be available to the estate, so IHT of £70,000 would be payable out of that (£400,000 less £225,000, at 40 per cent).

On lifetime gifts to companies or to any type of trusts, tax is payable when the gift is made at the reduced lifetime rate of 20 per cent, unless, when added to the running total of gifts in the preceding years, it falls within the nil-rate band:

- **If the person making the gift dies within seven years,** tax is recalculated at the death rates and any extra tax due is collected (though there may be some reduction where death occurs between three and seven years after making the gift – tapered relief (see box, right)). If the recalculation results in a lower tax bill, the tax already paid cannot be recovered.

Tapered relief

This relief applies where a person makes a PET in excess of the nil-rate band but then dies after at least three years. This also applies to chargeable gifts (e.g. gifts to trusts) where 20 per cent tax was paid at the time, but on the donor's death within seven years, tax is recalculated at the death rates. In such a case, the IHT due on the value of the gift will be reduced by:

- 20 per cent if the death occurs in the fourth year
- 40 per cent in the fifth year
- 60 per cent in the sixth year
- 80 per cent in the seventh year.

It is important to realise that this relief applies only to the amount by which the gift, when added to the total of gifts in the previous seven years, exceeds the nil-rate band.

If the gift falls within the nil-rate band, there will be no tapered relief because no tax is due.

Any tax that is due is paid by the person who received the gift. If the beneficiary can't (or won't) pay the bill, the sum comes out of the estate of the deceased donor.

 It can be possible to make IHT savings by writing a deed of variation after the testator has died. See pages 78–9 for a full explanation.

DISPOSING OF PROPERTY TO SAVE IHT

A lifetime gift of a parent's own main residence to a son or daughter is not an effective gift for saving IHT if there is any understanding that the parent is allowed to go on living there free of charge, because that amounts to 'reserving an interest'. However, giving away a house unconditionally and excluding the donor from benefiting in any way, or perhaps even a second home where the question of the giver remaining there would not even arise, could lead to considerable tax saving (but watch out for Capital Gains Tax (CGT) (see box, right) if you are thinking of giving away a second home).

A relatively new piece of legislation, known as the Pre-Owned Assets Tax (POAT), is now in existence. It stipulates that there should be an annual income tax charge on those who have divested themselves of assets (to reduce IHT liability), in circumstances in which they are still able to enjoy the assets that have been given away but the gift is not caught by the **reservation-of-benefit rules**. The charge is based on a notional income of 4.75 per cent as of 1 March 2009 of the value of the assets. It catches a number of tax-avoidance schemes but should not affect a situation in which a property is given away and the person giving it then pays a proper rent, or one in which a person gives a half-share in a property and the person receiving the gift moves in and shares the expenses. Although the new legislation is complicated, it cannot be

" POAT catches a number of tax-avoidance schemes but it should not affect a situation in which a property is given away and the person giving it remains in residence but pays a proper rent. "

Jargon buster

Reservation of interest Where a gift is made but the person making the gift continues to enjoy some benefit from the gifted property or asset, e.g. if you continue to live rent free in the house you have given away or if you give away a valuable picture but keep it hanging on your wall

! If an asset's value at the time you give it away is greater than its value at the time you first started to own it, you could be liable to pay Capital Gains Tax (CGT) on that difference. There are, however, exemptions and ways to mitigate this, so if you have any concerns, discuss the situation with your solicitor.

ignored by those seeking ways to avoid paying IHT. If you are thinking of giving your home to your children, but intend to continue living in it, take advice.

The changes to the IHT rules in 2008 make it possible for a person to make a will leaving their entire estate to their spouse or civil partner without wasting their nil-rate band. However, there can be several reasons why this is not a good idea. For example, your spouse or civil partner may be in a nursing home or you might have children from an earlier marriage who you will need to make special provisions for. Remember, the intestacy rules have not changed. If the estate is worth £325,000, without a will the surviving spouse or civil partner with children will only receive capital of £250,000, not £325,000 (see page 143 for further information).

OTHER WAYS OF SAVING IHT

There are other ways in which IHT may be saved, but these are more elaborate and beyond the scope of this book – see the *Which? Essential Guide* to *Giving and Inheriting* for more details.

One example is that it is possible to include a provision in a will whereby, for a period of two years after a person's death, the estate is held on trust for a class of people – usually 'my husband/wife and children', or 'my brothers and sisters' – and where the executors may, at their discretion, pay out the capital to any member of the class at any time within that period. This is called a 'two-year discretionary trust' and is

very flexible because the decision as to who will get what part of the property can be left for up to two years after the death, and it can therefore be used to obtain efficient tax treatment of a person's property at death but taking into account the needs at that time of any surviving spouse or civil partner. In this way (even though it may not be as efficient a distribution of property for IHT purposes as leaving it all to the children), the remaining spouse or civil partner can get the capital, or part of it, from the estate if or when he or she needs it, and the decision to pay it to him or her can be made at the last moment, thus preserving the possibility of at least reducing the tax burden.

! The government may revise these rules from time to time and may pass legislation that would severely restrict these possibilities. It is essential, therefore, to be up to date with legislation and any case law that may affect tax-avoidance schemes.

Trusts

A trust can be created by a will or lifetime gift. In the latter case, the terms of a trust are set out in the trust document and the trust begins on a chosen date. In the case of a trust created by a will, the trust begins on the date of the testator's death.

WHAT IS A TRUST?

Trusts can be created by will or by deed. Where money or other assets are held by trustees on behalf of a person or group of people, this is a trust, providing the following conditions apply:

- **The person creating the trust** must make his or her intention clear.
- **The money or assets to be held on trust** must be clearly defined.
- **The person or group of people** who are to benefit from the trust must be clear.

You might, for instance, use your will to create a trust for your infant children. The executors and trustees of your will would be the legal owners of the property or investments and, under the terms of the will, would be obliged to look after the property or investments on behalf of the infant children until the children reached 18 (or 21), at which time the investments would be transferred to the children.

Another common type of trust established by will is where the executors and trustees of the will hold property or investments in trust and pay the income to a beneficiary for his or her lifetime (known as the life tenant), after which the capital is to be paid to other beneficiaries (the remaindermen).

A variety of trusts can be created by a lifetime gift of assets or money, which will either be PETs, such as trusts for disabled beneficiaries, or untaxed because the amount given to the trustees is within the nil-rate band and, so, a possible way of avoiding IHT in the long term (for more on PETs, see page 31). As such, it is worth looking at any insurance or pensions policy you hold to see what happens to it if you die. There can be substantial IHT benefits if the money from the policy is paid into a discretionary trust rather than to your estate on your death.

Fixed trusts

These trusts set out, in fixed proportions, who gets what. Some flexibility can be introduced by giving the trustees wider powers, but their main advantage is their simplicity. They are easy to understand and relatively easy to administer.

Discretionary trusts

These set out who the potential beneficiaries may be (for example, wife, children and grandchildren), but give the trustees the discretion to decide what proportion of income and capital each beneficiary should receive (if any) and when they should receive it. The trustees do not have to pay anything out if they choose not to. Although the person creating the trust, the 'settlor', can tell the trustees how he or she would like them to exercise their discretion, the trustees are not legally bound by those wishes. The benefit of these trusts is in their flexibility, but the taxation provisions are somewhat complicated, so take advice.

Protective trusts

These trusts are used to provide for beneficiaries who may be profligate or are liable to be made bankrupt. Often what happens is that the beneficiary receives the income from the trust, but the payment of capital is subject to the discretion of the trustees.

Trusts for disabled beneficiaries

Special arrangements are permitted under the provisions of Section 89 of the Inheritance Tax Act 1984, which give favourable tax treatment to what are usually, in essence, discretionary trusts if the beneficiaries are, according to the Act, disabled, i.e. incapable of managing their affairs or in receipt of attendance allowance or disability living allowance.

WHO LOOKS AFTER THE TRUST?

A trust puts the legal ownership of property into the hands of – and under the control of – trustees, who act for the benefit of the beneficiaries of the trust and on the terms set out in the will or deed creating the trust. They are totally responsible for the administration of the property. So if you are creating a trust by deed or by will, think carefully about:

- **The choice of trustees** and any replacement.
- **The powers to be given to the trustees** and the duties imposed upon them.
- **Each trust has its own taxation regime**, so you must be aware of those that relate to the trust you have decided to establish.

The powers and obligations of trustees have, over the years, been carefully defined by law in order to protect the interests of the beneficiaries, but these can be varied by the deed or will (see also pages 47–8).

! The taxation of trusts is a subject in itself. If you are contemplating the creation of a lifetime trust, seek advice on the consequences of both IHT and CGT. Also investigate the income tax consequences.

Drafting your will

When drafting your will, there are a few legal necessities that must be adhered to in order to ensure it is legal. This chapter explains what these are, together with advice on choosing executors and trustees, what to think about when planning the distribution of your property and how a will should be set out, including important clauses.

The basics of making a will

Anyone can make a will provided that he or she is at least 18 years old and has testamentary capacity (that is, being able to appreciate the nature of the document he or she is signing, and its effect).

For your will to be valid, it must be:

- **In writing** (either handwritten or typed).
- **Signed by you.**
- **Signed in such a way** as to make absolutely clear your intention to give effect to the will. In other words, rather than signing it on the back or on the side of the will, you should sign it at the end of the writing on the final page.
- **Signed in the presence of two witnesses** (who must **not** be beneficiaries or potential beneficiaries under the will).

YOU MUST UNDERSTAND YOU ARE MAKING A WILL

There is no clear line between a person being capable of making a will and being incapable of doing so. The definition of testamentary mental capacity requires that you understand that you are making a will, know what you own and that the will distributes your property on your death. You must also be aware of those who might have claims or an expectation of inheriting on your death.

If there is a dispute later, medical evidence would be required to prove that this was the case (or not) at the time the will was made. The will can be made and signed in a lucid period during a psychiatric illness, although most hospitals and residential care homes have rules preventing nurses from witnessing the wills of patients. It is even possible for a person who is a patient under the Court of Protection to make a will.

It is one thing to remind an elderly parent that he or she should be making a will, but the whole process could be jeopardised if the will is written out by a main beneficiary, even if the witnesses were independent. This is because it could be suggested there had been undue influence or duress.

If the testator has good days and bad days, it is not always obvious whether some member of the family has been left out deliberately or as a result of forgetfulness.

If there are doubts about the mental capacity of a testator, the only safe way to proceed is to discuss the matter with the testator's medical adviser and for that adviser to be one of the witnesses when the will is signed. In practice it may not be as easy as that, especially where the testator is eccentric or mischievous.

Undue influence

It is one thing to have suspicions that a testator is being influenced to make a will benefiting one person at the expense of another, but it is much harder to produce solid evidence.

Undue influence could come in the form of gentle suggestions to a vulnerable testator or by physical threat. A common, and difficult, situation can arise when one member of the family living close to an elderly parent suggests that he or she should make a will. The elderly parent then makes a will but, in gratitude for the care being provided, gives everything to the person providing the care. To avoid suggestions of undue influence, it is probably wise to persuade the person making the will to visit a solicitor alone so that instructions can be given to an independent person.

Anyone wishing to challenge the will on the grounds that the testator was threatened or improperly influenced must show that the testator was induced to make the will by force, fear or fraud or that in some other way the will was not made voluntarily. If you think you are in this position, take legal advice before attempting to challenge a will on these grounds.

Where a will divides a testator's property, say, equally between his or her three children, it is unlikely, but not impossible, that there will be a dispute. However, where the testator attempts to vary the distribution of benefit, for example, based on the number of visits each child makes to the care home where he resides, there can be a bitter legacy for that family (see page 149).

If you are an executor and you believe that the testator lacked this mental capacity when making the will, you should proceed with caution. Seek medical evidence and legal advice. It can be very difficult to distinguish the will of a person lacking testamentary capacity from that of a deeply eccentric person.

❝ For a will to be valid, it must be in writing and signed by you and two witnesses in the presence of each other. ❞

For more information about signing and witnessing a will, together with an explanation of the necessity of an attestation clause, see pages 59-60.

DEFECTS

There are numerous reasons why a will can be defective. Some of these defects are fatal:

- The lack of witnesses.
- Undue influence.
- Lack of testamentary capacity.

Other defects, however, though not fatal, can cause problems after your death at the Probate Registry:

- Amended wills.
- The lack of an attestation clause, which is a clause explaining the process of signing and witnessing.
- The lack of a date.
- Unexplained marks or pinholes on the will.
- The lack of a legible name or full address for the witnesses.

Jargon buster

Assets The value of an estate
Beneficiary A person (or persons) who benefits from a will
Codicil A document altering an existing will
Executor A person responsible for dealing with your affairs after your death
Guardian A person who would become responsible for your children in the event of your death before your children are 18 years old
Testator The person making the will
Trustee A person responsible for administering a trust

THE STRUCTURE OF A WILL

There are no formal rules for writing a will, but it usually has four distinct sections:

1 **The appointment of executors** (and guardians if you have young children), and the revocation of any earlier wills (see pages 42–8).
2 **The distribution of your property** (that is, who is to have what after your death) and upon what terms. Legacies are usually fixed amounts, but the residue, where there are several beneficiaries, is distributed as a percentage or fraction of the whole (see pages 49–53).
3 **Any powers that the trustees will need** in order to carry out their duties properly, although many powers are supplied by existing Acts of Parliament, such as the Trustee Act 1925 and the Trustee Act 2000 (see pages 47–8).
4 **Directions,** such as arrangements for the funeral or the terms on which a person can live in a house (see pages 54–8).

Use simple language and avoid any expressions that are vague and ambiguous or which you do not fully understand (see box, opposite).

It has been customary practice for solicitors and will writers to include a comprehensive list of powers and administrative provisions in the will even when some of those provisions were automatically included by statute with the result that the will became clogged up with administrative provisions making it difficult for the layman to understand what the will was actually saying.

This problem has been tackled by the Society of Trust and Estate Practitioners (STEP), who have prepared a set of standard administrative provisions that can be incorporated by reference into the body of a will without having to set them out in full (see page 68 for details). Having said that, it may still be necessary to vary or add to those standard provisions in particular cases.

Vague or ambiguous words

It may seem obvious to say so, but you must watch for ambiguous language. The following are examples of the sorts of thing you should avoid:

- 'I give £1,000 to my nephews.' Do you mean £1,000 each or £1,000 to be divided between them?
- 'I give my house to my daughter and the adjoining barn to my son.' You may know where the dividing line is to be and who should own the driveway, but do they?
- 'I give all my money to my friend Jack.' Do you mean the cash in the house, all your investments apart from your house, or everything you own when it has been sold? And is it clear which friend Jack you are referring to? To help prevent such confusion, it is always best to give a full name and current address.

❝A serious defect in a will renders it void. The most serious defects include a lack of witnesses, the testator having been unduly influenced and lack of testamentary capacity.❞

Appointing representatives

Choosing an executor, guardian and/or trustee is a serious business.
They need to have an orderly approach to problems and be trustworthy.

EXECUTORS

An executor is responsible for administering all the affairs of your estate when you die. Executors should always be appointed by will. If the will does not appoint an executor, your next of kin will usually be appointed by the intestacy rules for administering your estate; they are then called the administrators. Executors and administrators are both personal representatives, but executors have the power to deal with the affairs of the testator (the person making the will) from the moment of death whereas administrators have no such authority and must theoretically wait for the registry to grant them letters of administration before being able to take any action. This can present problems if there is a dispute about who is to make the funeral arrangements or if certain members of the family start going through your possessions without the agreement of others equally entitled to them.

Once the administration of an estate has been completed by realising the

 An executor, so long as he or she is not guilty of any misconduct, cannot be forced to renounce or retire. It could therefore be difficult, but not impossible, to persuade a bank to relinquish its executorship even if one or more members of the family are joint executors with the bank and could act quite satisfactorily without the bank.

assets, paying the taxes and debts and distributing the residue, the executor's job is finished. He or she may, however, continue to work as a trustee if, for instance, some of the money has to be retained for minors until they reach 18 (see page 47).

 The distinction made between an executor and administrator is further explained on pages 88-9 in Administering an estate.

What executors do

Executors' duties are no mere formalities; there is a great deal of work involved. They are responsible for:

- **Collecting in all the assets** of the estate.
- **Dealing with the paperwork** and calculations.
- **Paying all the debts,** liabilities and taxes and the various expenses, such as funeral costs and administration costs.
- **Distributing all the property** that remains in the estate in accordance with the terms of the will – paying the legacies, transferring particular items of property to the beneficiaries, paying out the residue of the estate to one or more specified beneficiaries, or holding the property 'in trust' on the terms specified in the testator's will.

If they misinterpret the will or a specific tax law, they can become personally liable for someone else's loss.

❝ When you die, your executors are responsible for administering your estate. If you don't appoint them by writing a will, your next of kin will be appointed as administrators. ❞

Who to appoint

You cannot force someone to take on the duties of being your executor, so it is much better to ask the people you have in mind first if they agree to be appointed. An executor may not really wish to act but may feel duty-bound to do so when the time comes, because he or she has been appointed. You should therefore try to find someone who you know would be willing to act and capable of doing so.

In normal circumstances, a husband will appoint his wife to be his executor and vice versa, especially where they do not have grown-up children. This is a good idea, as a rule, because the surviving partner will usually be receiving most of the estate, so it is sensible that he or she should have a hand in its administration.

It is perhaps as well, though, that a wife/husband should not be the only executor. She (let us say) will have enough to cope with at the time of her husband's death without this. Alternatively there may, of course, be some common accident. Who to choose as the other executor should depend largely on the circumstances of the people concerned. The maximum number of executors allowed is four but you can appoint reserves.

- **If there are children who are minors,** it may be sensible to have a professional person, for example, a solicitor or an accountant, to act because the property will subsequently have to be held in trust for the children, although there is no reason why the trustee should not be a trusted friend of the family. There should normally be at least two trustees where children are involved.

- **If the children have attained their majority,** one or other of the children can be a joint executor. Often the grown-up children are the only executors. It is normal to appoint at least two executors where the will creates a continuing trust, for example for children.

It is usually preferable to select as an executor a person who is younger than you. It is also sensible to provide in your will for a substitute executor in case the first people you appoint are unwilling or unable to act, or in case they die before you do. If an executor is not a member of the immediate family and not someone who is a professional, and is therefore undertaking the duties as a trusted friend, it is sometimes thought appropriate to leave him or her a legacy

(£1,000, say) for undertaking the office of executor. Otherwise, executors are only entitled to recover expenses but nothing for the time they have spent on the job.

When a solicitor or other professional is appointed to be an executor, it is normal to include a clause in your will enabling him or her to charge normal professional fees for the legal work in administering the estate, although the Trustee Act 2000 allows a professional trustee to charge reasonable fees if the co-executors agree. There is no obligation or presumption that a solicitor should be given a legacy for acting as an executor.

> **❝ If an executor undertakes the duties as a trusted friend, it is often thought appropriate to leave him or her a legacy by way of a thank you. ❞**

When you own a business

If you own a business or are perhaps a writer with literary assets, it will be wise to appoint executors who have the knowledge to run the business while it is being sold or to dispose of your literary assets to the best advantage. The will should also give appropriate powers to enable executors to carry out these tasks and remuneration to compensate them for doing so.

Appointing a bank

A bank can act as an executor of your will. You may wish to consider appointing a bank if there is no one individual to whom you feel you could entrust this task, maybe because there are family arguments. However, the disadvantages of having a bank as an executor include the fact that the costs of administration of the estate will usually be considerably more than those of professional trustees and executors, such as accountants and solicitors. Also, banks do not always have the personal knowledge of the family that an individual appointed by you would usually have. There are likely to be some tasks that require the personal touch, such as sorting out the personal belongings of the person who has died, for instance. Banks may employ competent and sympathetic staff, but they are no substitute for the right friend or relation.

Sometimes a bank is appointed to be an executor jointly with an individual, perhaps a member of the family or a close friend. When the time comes to administer the estate, the individual executor may feel quite capable of doing so himself without the assistance of the bank, but if the estate is large, it is very unlikely that the bank would agree to renounce its role and therefore its fee.

If you are considering appointing any commercial organisation, including a bank, as your executor, examine its literature and publicity, and in particular the rates of charging for administering the estate, including additional items, such as acceptance fees, arrangement fees, annual management fees and withdrawal fees. Work out how much it will cost, especially if the administration is likely to be straightforward. If you are leaving

everything to your spouse or civil partner and adult children, it may not be necessary to use the bank at all. Some banks charge a fee of 4 per cent on the first £250,000 of the estate (and some 4 per cent on the first £500,000) with a decreasing scale for the remainder. In straightforward cases, it is probably better to appoint individuals to be your executors if suitable candidates are willing to act.

> **❝ Banks may employ competent and sympathetic staff, but they are no substitute for the right friend or relation. ❞**

GUARDIANS

You can state in your will who you wish to take on the obligations and liabilities of bringing up your children if they were orphaned, rather than leaving it to the court to decide who is the most suitable person. For anyone with young children it is sensible to appoint a guardian (or guardians). Under the provisions of the Children Act 1989, a person must have parental responsibility before he or she can appoint a guardian for a child. The father of an illegitimate child cannot appoint a guardian unless he already has parental responsibility. If the father does not have parental responsibility, legal advice must be sought if he wishes to make a will appointing a guardian.

> **!** If you are going to appoint a bank to be the executor of your will, you should use the appointment clause supplied by the bank.

If either the father or mother of a child dies, the survivor will usually be responsible for bringing up the children, although unmarried fathers should ensure they have been granted parental responsibility. However, on the death of the survivor or following some common accident in which both parents die within a short time of each other, the appointment of guardians will become necessary. Generally, such guardianship issues would arise only after the death of both parents.

Choosing the guardians of your children

This obviously requires careful consideration. The main issues are to do with the personal qualities of the friends or relatives you wish your children to be brought up by, and also their ability in financial matters.

If the appointment of guardians takes effect, the estate of the deceased person will almost always be held in trust for the children and its income can be used for their maintenance. It is worth considering, therefore, whether to make the guardians executors and trustees as well. It may not

be a good idea to make them the only executors and trustees. Perhaps a professional (for example, a solicitor or accountant) should join them as a trustee to intervene if there is any risk of a conflict of interest. He or she can also help with the formalities of the administration and investment of the money if the guardians are kept busy by the day-to-day care of the children.

" Generally, guardianship issues would arise only after the death of both parents. Who you choose to act as guardian depends on the personal qualities of friends or relatives. "

Providing monetary support

Potential guardians will obviously want to know if any money will be available to meet the cost of maintaining the children, otherwise they might not be able to afford to take on the responsibility. Sometimes the testator will set down a formula for calculating how much money should be paid to a guardian for looking after the children, for instance by linking it to the local authority payments to foster parents.

TRUSTEES

Trustees are people who legally own and administer property for the benefit of others (called the beneficiaries). They are not usually allowed to benefit from that property themselves in their capacity as trustees, but they can be both trustee and beneficiary within the same trust.

The job of a trustee is to manage the property for the benefit of the beneficiaries under the terms of the trust and in accordance with the law. For example, a trust arises where property is given to children under the age of 18 (see pages 35–6). The trustees of the will or deed hold the property for the benefit of the children until they reach the age of 18 or later. The terms on which the property is held in trust are set out in the document setting up the trust (which can be a will) or by various Acts of Parliament.

People are sometimes puzzled to find one person who is both trustee and beneficiary. It might be explained as the wearing of two hats – there is the trustee hat, under which you must observe all the obligations placed on you as a trustee by the will and by statute; and the beneficiary hat, under which you

> If the beneficiaries are of full age and they are absolutely entitled to all the property held on their behalf by a trustee, they can compel the retirement of that trustee.

are entitled to a certain share of the estate of the deceased or trust assets.

The powers of trustees

The law provides automatic powers for the trustees of your will to enable them to carry out their duties. The main ones are the following:

- **The power of advancement.** This allows trustees to pay capital to an infant beneficiary (or spend it on him or her) who has not yet reached the age when he or she becomes absolutely entitled. The advancement is limited to one-half of the beneficiary's expected share.
- **The powers of appropriation.** This enables the trustees to pass over shares or property in order to satisfy a legacy or bequest without selling them and handing over the cash.
- **The power to run the testator's business.** This enables the executors/ trustees, while they try to sell the business as a going concern, to run it for up to a year.
- **The power of trustees to charge.** Under the Trustee Act 2000, 'trust corporations' and professional trustees with the consent of the other executors may charge for work done, even where the will does not contain a charging clause. Generally, a trustee cannot charge for work done as a trustee but can recover expenses.
- **The power to delegate.** Trustees may delegate their administrative powers but they may not delegate their powers of distribution.

- **Insurance.** The trustees have power to insure the trust property.
- **Investment.** While the Trustee Act 2000 gives wide powers of investment to the trustees, it also places them under a duty to obtain and consider proper investment advice and to review their investments each year. The adviser must be suitably qualified with appropriate expertise and subject to a professional code of conduct.

In particular circumstances, you may feel that further powers are needed by your trustees, including the extension of some of their statutory powers (see box, below).

Any other powers you want to give to your executors and trustees should be set out in your will. The following additional trustee powers are often found in wills:

- **The power to postpone the sale** of property held on trust.
- **The power to advance all the capital** to benefit beneficiaries in satisfaction of their **contingent** interest – for example, where someone is entitled to payment at the age of 21, this power enables the trustees to make the payment at any time from 18 onwards if they think fit (perhaps to pay university fees).

Jargon buster

Contingent Where an event must happen before a gift can be made, e.g. the beneficiary must reach 21 before any payment can be made. The 18-year-old therefore has a contingent rather than an absolute entitlement to the money

- **Wide powers of investment,** including the right to invest in non-income-producing assets, such as insurance policies.
- **The specific power to carry on your business** for longer than a year.
- **Additional power to borrow or lend** (with or without charging interest).
- **The power to use income or capital** to improve trust property.
- **The power to sell assets** to beneficiaries who are also trustees.

 A comprehensive set of powers and provisions for trustees has been prepared by the Society of Trust and Estate Practitioners (STEP). See page 68 for details.

Distributing your property

Before deciding who you wish to benefit from your will, and if you haven't done so already, set down a rough calculation of your estate and what it is worth as outlined on page 19. Now read this section, which describes different ways in which you can distribute your property.

LEGACIES

Legacies are usually particular items or fixed sums of money.

Make a note of the people to whom you wish to give any legacies, including, possibly, a friend who has agreed to act as executor. List any particular items you want to leave to special people – for example, your wedding ring to your granddaughter, or the piano to your nephew. If the gifts are valuable, make a note of their likely value. You may wish to give money to a few of your friends, relations, godchildren or people who have been especially helpful to you in some way or other (for example, £100 to the child of an old friend).

You can also give a sum of money to a class of people, for example, '£500 to each of my brothers and sisters living at my death', or one particular sum of money, for example, '£2,000 to be divided equally between all my grandchildren living at my death'. Avoid gifts to a class of people that may not be known for many years, for example, 'to all my grandchildren'. You may have a son aged 30 who fathers a child when he is 60. If you die soon after making your will, your executors would have to wait at least 30 years to be sure that all the

grandchildren had been born. It is unwise to leave money in a specific bank account to a beneficiary as a legacy because the account may have changed or the bank may have been taken over by another bank before your death.

It is important to specify carefully the class of people whom you wish to benefit and to specify, for example:

- **Whether it excludes illegitimate children** or includes stepchildren and whether your husband's brother's sons are covered by the word 'nephew' in your will. (For these purposes, there is no legal distinction between children born in wedlock and adopted children.)
- **Are the husbands of aunts** included in the word 'uncles' or does it mean the brothers of parents only?
- **Does the term 'nephew'** include illegitimate nephews?

❝Legacies are usually particular items or fixed sums of money. ❞

If there is any doubt at all, it is better to list people by their names. If the person to whom the legacy is made dies before you, the gift will lapse (be cancelled) unless your will says otherwise or that person is your descendant with children of their own, in which case the children (your grandchildren) will share their parents' legacy.

If you are giving a house to someone

It is important to decide what should happen to any mortgage that is outstanding. Is the gift subject to it or is the mortgage debt to be repaid from the residue of your estate? It may be that the mortgage debt is covered by an insurance policy so that the mortgage would automatically be repaid on your death. Be careful to check whether the insurance policy will be paid direct to the mortgage company or, as part of the residue, to your executors. If your will does not make the situation crystal clear, you may find that your will has left a house subject to a mortgage to one beneficiary while the proceeds of the endowment policy (intended to pay off the mortgage) actually pass to someone else.

❝ If you are giving to charity, give an alternative in case the charity no longer exists when you die. ❞

Charitable legacies

You may wish to give a sum to charity. Often people leave a sum of money to a charity with which they have been concerned in their life. A particular friend or relative may have benefited from a heart research foundation or leukaemia fund, for example, so you might wish to make a donation to that particular charity. It is very important to get the name, address and charity number of the charity correct, otherwise the gift could be invalidated. It is also wise to give an alternative, in case the charity no longer exists at the date of your death.

! Remember that the will is operative only from the date of your death. If you leave someone a particular item of jewellery, a house or any other property by will, but then you dispose of it before your death, the beneficiary will not receive that item of property.

THE REST OF YOUR ESTATE (THE RESIDUE)

It is impossible to specify the amount of money that will go to the residuary beneficiary/beneficiaries. Even if this could be calculated at today's date, it would certainly not be correct on your death in, say, ten years' time. All you can do, therefore, is to specify who is to receive the rest of your estate and, if more than one person, in what proportions. The lawyers call it 'residue' and the term 'residuary estate' is everything that is left after all the debts, liabilities, taxes, costs and legacies have been paid or transferred. The residue can go to one person, or to a number of people in equal or unequal shares.

It is usual to include a term in the will stating that 'all debts, testamentary expenses and Inheritance Tax (IHT) are to be paid from the residue'. When making a will, you should be clear about your debts and set down how they are to be paid in the event of your death.

Absolute or life interest gift?

When disposing of the residue of your estate you will have to decide if you wish the main beneficiaries of your estate to have the property (meaning the capital of your estate) outright – an absolute gift – that is, without any condition whatever. Alternatively, you might wish them to receive the income, but not the capital, for the rest of their lives so that the capital can then pass on their death to someone else you have chosen – a life interest gift. It is most usual for people to

❝When making your will, be clear about your debts and set down how they are to be paid in the event of your death.❞

give their property outright, that is, to make an absolute gift.

In the case of a life interest gift, bear in mind that the beneficiary with the life interest will only be entitled to the income from the property during his (or her) life. He or she will be entitled to the interest and/or dividends on the money or investments, and will be able to have the use of any property that does not earn income, such as a house. In such a case, the beneficiary could rent out the house and receive the rent. (There can be complications as to repair, maintenance and outgoings of a house where the interest is limited in this way.) In this instance, the right wording is extremely important as you may establish either:

- A right to reside in a house with no continuing benefits if the beneficiary moves out or
- A life interest, where you are giving the beneficiary the right to use the house or to sell it and enjoy the income generated by the resulting capital for the rest of that person's life.

After your death, during the period of the life interest (see pages 30–1), there will be the costs of administering the estate, completing Income Tax returns and trust accounts to look after, so you may wish to appoint a professional executor.

If you have provided that the residue should be invested and only the income paid to someone (your spouse or civil partner, perhaps, during his or her life), the capital would have to be protected by your trustees until the death of the life tenant, when it would be divided between the '**remaindermen**' who share the property when the life tenant dies. These matters can be important where you wish to guarantee that the capital passes the way you want it to rather than allowing your spouse or civil partner to make that decision. It may be even more important where, for example, you have children from a previous marriage, or if you are living with a partner to whom you are not married and you wish him or her to be provided for, for life, but also to guarantee that your children benefit from your property after the death of your present partner.

> **❝ If a beneficiary dies before you and is not your descendant, your gift will lapse. ❞**

IF A BENEFICIARY WERE TO DIE BEFORE YOU

You should think about this when planning your will, even if the beneficiary is much younger than you. Generally, if the beneficiary dies before you and is not your descendant, your gift will lapse. If you want the gift to go to his or her spouse or child in the event of his or her death before yours, you should say so in your will. However, if a son or daughter of yours who is destined to receive something under your will dies before you, leaving a child, the gift you had intended to leave to the son or daughter will automatically go to that son or daughter's child unless you make specific provision that it should not do so.

In the case of a cash legacy, such as '£100 to John Brown' or a specific bequest such as 'my diamond brooch to Jane Smith', no problem arises – if John Brown or Jane Smith is dead, the gift will become part of the residue and swell the amount that will go to the person who is to receive your residuary estate.

If the person who is to receive the residue of your estate dies before you (and is not your descendant), that would leave part of your property undisposed of. This is called **partial intestacy** as the lapsed share is then dealt with under the intestacy provisions. It is therefore wise to name an alternative if your will provides for only one residuary beneficiary.

If, however, a beneficiary were to die after you but before the bequest is actually paid to him or her, the beneficiary's estate will receive that money – it would not go back into your residuary estate.

TRYING TO DISINHERIT A DEPENDANT

When deciding who should benefit, most people naturally favour the members of their own immediate family, and this is a notion that the law encourages. Although you are free to give all your assets to anyone you specify in your will, certain people who are closely related to you in one way or another and whom you have supported can, regardless of the terms of your will, make an application to the court for a share in your estate. If, for any reason, you decide that your spouse or civil partner or any of your children or anyone else financially dependent on you should inherit little or nothing under your will after your death, any one of them could apply to the court for reasonable provision to be made for them out of what you have left. The same rules apply if someone has been left out because of the intestacy rules (your cohabitee, for example) (see pages 11–12).

There are circumstances in which such people can properly be excluded from benefiting from your estate, for example, because a spouse or civil partner has already been given a house and large sum during your lifetime, or is financially wholly independent.

To prevent people from making successful claims against your will, make sure the wording is clear and well thought out – consult a solicitor. Alternatively, you could consider making a bequest to people who might make such a claim as they might be less likely to claim if they have been given something rather than nothing at all.

❝ Although you are free to give all your assets to anyone you specify in your will, family members you have supported can make an application to the court for a share in your estate. ❞

Other issues

There are other clauses that you might want to include in your will or think about when you are drawing up your will. They are outlined here for you to consider and then discuss with your solicitor.

DIRECTIONS TO YOUR EXECUTORS

This is a bit of a 'catch-all' section in your will and some typical directions are:

- **Advance payments.** You can state: 'If any beneficiary in my will has received a gift or advance payment from me, no account of that gift or advance shall be taken when ascertaining the entitlement of that beneficiary.' Or, conversely, 'If any beneficiary in my will has received a gift or advance from me, that gift or advance shall be taken into account with/without interest when ascertaining the entitlement of that beneficiary.'
- **Foreign property.** If you have made a foreign will disposing of foreign property, make clear in your UK will what property is covered by the foreign will and remember not to revoke all earlier wills (see revocation clause on page 56).
- **Funeral arrangements.** If these are complicated, write out detailed instructions so your executors know what you want. The will can then state your preference for burial or cremation (see below).
- **Donation of your body for medical research** (see opposite).
- **Donation of organs for transplantation** (see opposite).

Funeral arrangements

If any particular arrangements are required – your wishes for burial in a particular plot or for your ashes to be scattered in a specific place – set these out in the will.

> **❝ Specific instructions to your executors can include funeral arrangements and organ and body donation. ❞**

 For more information on making funeral arrangements, see the *Which? Essential Guide* to *What to do When Someone Dies*.

Donation of body for medical research

A number of people express the wish that their body should be used after death for medical research. Bodies donated in this way are used by doctors and medical students who are studying and researching the structure and function of the normal human body. If you wish to do this and would like more information, go to www.doh.gov.uk and key HTA (Human Tissue Authority) into the search box.

Alternatively, make arrangements with your chosen medical school or hospital direct. These organisations provide the necessary documentation and a contact address for your executors. It is always wise to tell your executors of the arrangements so they can act quickly in the event of your death.

Organ donation for transplantation

Organ transplantation is one of the greatest medical success stories of our time. Kidney, liver, heart and heart-lung transplants have now become routine operations, and the process is constantly being developed. In the UK in 2005, 2,796 patients had their lives saved or improved by organ transplantation.

The overall effectiveness of the transplant programme is limited by the fact that the demand for organs still far exceeds their availability. Today, nearly 7,000 people in the UK are registered for an organ transplant, most for a kidney but others for a heart, liver or lungs. However, still fewer than 3,000

Living wills

If you want to avoid a situation where you are incurably ill or severely incapacitated and are not able to refuse treatment that is keeping you alive, you can make a 'living will', which will express your wishes in the event of this happening.

In particular, the living will can express your wishes on receiving treatment that might ease your suffering even though it would not prolong your life. It might also instruct your doctors to withhold or withdraw certain treatments that could keep you alive. It would be sensible to discuss such a will with your doctor before completing it. The law has changed recently with the birth of Lasting Powers of Attorney (Welfare) and Advance Directives. Details are outside the scope of this Essential Guide.

A number of organisations, including the Natural Death Centre, can provide further information on living wills (see box, below).

 For more information about the Natural Death Centre go to their website at www.naturaldeath.org.uk.

If organ donation is your wish, it is very important that you inform your family and friends, so that they are in no doubt should the time ever come.

transplants are carried out each year: last year almost 500 people died while awaiting a transplant.

The NHS UK Transplant keeps an Organ Donor Register (see box, below), which is a confidential, computerised record of the wishes of people who have decided that, after their death, they want to leave a legacy of life for others.

❝ Even if you haven't made a will before, include the revocation clause because your executors then needn't worry about looking for an earlier will. ❞

REVOCATION CLAUSE

There is one clause that should always be included in a will (unless you have made a foreign will disposing of property abroad), namely one saying that 'any previous wills are revoked'. A later will does not automatically revoke an earlier one. If a person leaves two wills and parts of them are consistent with each other, they stand together; where the wills are inconsistent, the later one prevails; but having two wills is almost always likely to cause problems.

Even if you have not made a will before, it is a good idea to include a statement that previous wills are revoked because your executors might wonder, after your death, whether perhaps you left an earlier will. Having a revocation clause in your will saves your executors a fruitless search for any earlier will by showing that it is revoked anyway.

There is, however, one exception: when you make a will before you get married, you can provide that the will should remain valid after your marriage even though marriage normally invalidates an existing will.

SURVIVORSHIP CLAUSE

It is possible for a husband and wife or civil partners to die as a result of some joint accident so that one of them survives the other for only a few days or weeks. He or she will then have inherited

 If you want to look further into organ donation, information is available at www.uktransplant.org.uk or phone the organ donor line on 0845 60 60 400 to obtain a free leaflet entitled *Organ Donation, Your Questions Answered.*

the property without any opportunity to enjoy it.

For that reason, a husband and wife may wish to leave their property to the other with the proviso that, in order to inherit, the survivor survives for at least, say, 30 days. If the survivor dies within that period, the property does not go to the survivor but will pass directly to, say, the children or whoever else is specified by the will.

The stipulated survival time (known as a survivorship clause) could be some other number of days. However, 30 days is usually chosen because if the survivor survives for more than 30 days, the chances are that he or she will have some independent life after the deceased and should therefore benefit from inheriting the property.

In cases where IHT is payable (see pages 29–34), such a clause may not be a good idea, although the doubling of the IHT allowance has simplified matters. For example, suppose that a husband is worth £500,000 but his wife is worth £100,000 and their wills leave everything to the survivor provided she or he survives him or her by 30 days, otherwise everything goes to the children. If he dies and she follows him a week later, £60,000 of IHT will be payable in his estate and £0 in hers. Without the survivorship clause, no IHT would have been payable in either estate

The decision to include or exclude a survivorship clause must depend on the tax planning of each person's estate. Tread carefully where there is a possible liability of IHT.

❝The stipulated survival time is usually 30 days, however it could be fewer if necessary.❞

(because she would have inherited everything on his death and on hers everything would have fallen into the nil-rate band of £650,000).

It may be possible to rescue this situation with a Deed of Variation (see page 78), but this can be an expensive process if the children are minors or there are trusts in the wills.

See page 65 for a typical wording of the revocation clause. For other ways to revoke a will, see pages 80-2.

POWER OF ATTORNEY

Although your will says what should happen to your estate on your death, it is worth considering what would happen to your property if you became incapable, through age or infirmity, of managing your own affairs. This happens more frequently with increasing life expectancy leading to a greater incidence of dementia. Until 1985, your spouse or family (or local authority) would have had to apply to the Court of Protection for an order authorising him or her to deal with your financial affairs under the supervision of that Court. This is inconvenient.

Since 1985, however, it has been possible to give another person the authority to look after your affairs without the expense of applying to the Court of Protection and of the subsequent supervision. In 1985, it became possible to appoint one or two such people to handle your affairs on your behalf. This was done by signing an Enduring Power of Attorney (EPA). Since 2007, the procedure has changed and become more complicated. The document is now called a Lasting Power of Attorney (LPA) (Property).

Old EPAs remain valid and it is generally a bad idea to replace one by a new LPA unless you need to. Circumstances that might make this a necessity would be because the persons named as attorneys have died, become incapable or unwilling, or you have changed your mind about who can trust to fulfil this role.

An EPA or LPA is usually a more satisfactory way of arranging for your affairs to be dealt with in case of incapacity. Leaving it to someone to apply to the Court of Protection to be appointed to administer your affairs (called a Deputy) is troublesome, expensive and can be contentious.

Lasting Power of Attorney

There are two types of Lasting Power of Attorney (LPA) (each having a £150 registration fee). One covers finance and property and the other covers health and welfare. The rules and procedures for LPAs are intended to give protection to vulnerable people under the jurisdiction of the Court of Protection. They are administered by the Office of the Public Guardian.

 Forms, and much useful information is available on the website of the Office of the Public Guardian at www.publicguardian.gov.uk.

Finishing your will

Once you have decided on the contents of your will, go to your solicitor or will writer. Whichever method you use, you must observe the strict rules that apply to the signing of a will. The attestation clause is a helpful and necessary reminder.

ATTESTATION CLAUSE

The will should contain an attestation clause, that is, a clause explaining the process of signing and witnessing. If the clause were missing, then, after the testator's death, when it comes to proving the will, it would be necessary to have an affidavit – a sworn statement – from one of the witnesses to explain what happened when the will was signed and witnessed. This could cause great difficulties if the witnesses could not be traced, or were dead.

The Principal Probate Registry and the District Registries will accept the following attestation clause:

'Signed by the testator in our presence and attested by us in his/her presence and in the presence of each other'

If you are blind, the attestation clause must say that the will was read to you and that, having stated that you understood it, you signed it or, alternatively, it was signed on your behalf. Appropriate variations have to be made for illiterate testators (who cannot read) or physically disabled testators (who may not be able to read or write).

SIGNING AND WITNESSES

The will must be signed first by the testator (the person whose will it is) within the sight of two witnesses who should both be present together when the testator actually signs. The witnesses should then both sign in the presence of the testator and of each other.

The witnesses must both be present when you sign and must then 'attest' and sign the will themselves. It is also advisable for you and your witnesses to sign at the bottom of each page.

It is not strictly necessary for the witnesses to write their addresses on the will. Their signature is all that is legally required. But it is much better if they do add their addresses, and perhaps their occupations as well, so that if there were any questions raised later about what happened at the time, they could more easily be traced. For the same reason, it is a good idea to write the witnesses' names in block letters underneath their signatures, especially where the signatures are hard to read.

No one who is left anything in the will (or their husband or wife) should be a witness. Where this happens, the will is still legally valid – in other words, these witnesses are perfectly all right as witnesses, but they lose their legacies or benefits. The will is interpreted as if the gift to the witness, or the spouse or civil partner of the witness, were cut out of it. Similarly, a person appointed as executor should not really be a witness. If he or she is, the will is valid and so is the appointment, but any legacy or gift to the executor would not be.

A blind person cannot be a witness. Also it is probably more sensible to avoid having someone under the age of 18 to be a witness, though there is nothing in the law to prevent it.

> **!** Do not pin or clip anything to your will and make sure that no pin holes appear in it. Such holes, or marks where a paper clip has been attached, may give the impression that a sheet of paper forming part of your will was at one time attached to it but has now disappeared.

The date of a will

A will should be dated with the date on which it is signed in order to be valid. If not, there will be a problem obtaining probate and deciding on priority if there is another will in existance. The date can appear at the beginning or at the end. There is no need to set out the date in an extravagant way. To say 'in the year of Our Lord ...' is unnecessary: you could simply put '27 November 2009', provided it is written legibly in the space on the will meant for it. The date should be put in when the will is finally signed in the presence of the witnesses.

When the will is long

If your will runs to more than one page, sign each page at the bottom immediately after the last line of writing, without leaving any gap, and ask the witnesses to do the same. This is not a legal requirement, but it does help to prevent any forgery of your will.

The form of your will

Countless attempts have been made to prepare standard will forms to cover what might be called 'typical cases'. Unfortunately, one typical case is seldom exactly like another typical case, so standard will forms are best avoided. The will of an aspiring bachelor of 26 will have different priorities from the will of a single mother on benefits or the will of a 43-year-old father of three.

To help you see how the form of your will might take shape, think about your circumstances and wishes as outlined on pages 20–8 and answer the questions overleaf.

 You should review your will every few years and more frequently if there are big events in your life, such as a marriage or children. It is possible to make small changes by codicil (see pages 77–8) but, even then, it may be better to make a completely new will if circumstances require any changes.

WILL OF A HUSBAND/WIFE WITH YOUNG CHILDREN

If you are a married couple and have young children, it is usual for each of you to make a will in similar terms and at the same time because you cannot know which of you is going to die first and how long there will be between your two deaths. Both of you should make provision for what is to happen if the other dies first. The wills should, therefore, be broadly in the same form. (*continued on page 64*)

❝One typical case is seldom like another typical case, so there is no such thing as a 'standard' will.❞

It is nigh on impossible to have a standard will, but to help you get started, an example will for a married couple with children is provided on pages 65–6 together with detailed notes on the following pages.

Drafting your will: a checklist

The points described below are the most common and important matters that you must bear in mind when drafting your will.

Executors

Do you know who they will be? Are they willing to act for you? Are they younger than you (it is best that they should be, to avoid the risk of intestacy)? (See pages 42-5.)

Guardians

If you have infant children and you die, who will look after them? Would your chosen guardian have enough money to care for them as you would like? How much do you think they should be paid for looking after your children (who might be 3 or 17 at the time)? (See pages 45-6.)

Beneficiaries

Who are they? Are they under 18? If so, do you want to give the executors power to release money to them before they reach 18 (or 21)? (See pages 49-53.)

Foreign property

Do you own any? If so, you should make a will in that country to deal with it. If you have already done so, do not negate that will accidentally by using the normal revocation clause in your UK will (see page 56). Civil partnership may not be recognised in some countries.

Trusts

Are there any existing trusts that might affect IHT on your estate? In any case, it may be sensible to create a trust yourself through your will. (See pages 35-6.)

Gifts

Have you made any gifts in your lifetime that qualify as potentially exempt transfers (PETs)? Have you made any gifts that do not qualify as PETs because you have retained an interest or benefit? (See pages 31-2.)

IHT

Is there any way to avoid or reduce IHT? (See pages 33-4.) If you are cohabiting, you could save over £100,000 by getting married or entering into a civil partnership.

Claims against your estate

Is there a chance of any claims being made if you leave someone out? Should you include an explanation for any exclusion?

Automatic transfer of property

What property automatically changes hands irrespective of what your will says? For example, do you own your house as a joint tenant? Do you have insurance policies written in trust for your spouse or civil partner and children? (See pages 23-4.)

Specific items

Are there any you want to leave to a particular person? (See pages 49-50.)

Specific sums of money

Are there any you want to leave to a particular person? (See pages 49-50.)

Residue of your estate

What do you want to happen to it? (See pages 51-2.)

Your body

Do you have any specific wishes? Do you want it buried, cremated, given for medical research or donated for transplants? (See pages 54-6.)

Pets

If you have any, what is to happen to them? (See page 28.)

In addition to the items included on the checklist on pages 62–3, you need to think about:

- What should happen if you both die together, for example, in an accident (see page 20–1).
- Whether you should transfer any assets to your children, or step-children if you have any, to prevent them losing out at a later stage should you divorce your spouse or civil partner or need permanent nursing care later in life.
- If there is a mortgage protection policy, ensure that it will be held on trust for the survivors and will not form part of your estate (see page 24).
- Whether you should take out a term insurance policy, which would run, say, for 20 years, to protect the family if either of you should die in that period.

If the policy were written in trust for the survivor, it would not form part of the estate of the deceased.

- Who the residue will pass to (in this instance, it is usually the spouse or civil partner or, in the event of the death of the spouse or civil partner before the testator, the residue is held for the children by the executors (as trustees) until they reach a minimum age of 18).

You can both provide for a number of situations that may or may not arise over the next few years. You can also revoke or alter the will at any time before your death. Although you should be aware of the tax consequences of your will, do not allow the desire for tax avoidance to prevent a proper provision for your spouse or civil partner in the event of your death. Ensure you consider all the likely events.

Children from a previous marriage

If either of you has children from a previous relationship or marriage as well as children by your current spouse, the preparation of a will is essential. In such cases, you might include a discretionary trust in your will (see pages 35–6) to deal with the circumstances arising at the time of your death that cannot be anticipated when you are making your will. Whatever you do, you have a dilemma:

If you leave everything to your spouse so your infant children will be looked after, it will be up to your spouse to make a will that provides for the children of your first marriage as well as the second. If the surviving spouse remarries or changes their will, the children of the first marriage may get nothing.

Alternatively, if you give your surviving spouse a life interest in your estate and the capital on his or her death to be divided between all your children, you will ensure that your children benefit but the income from that capital may not be enough to provide for your spouse and to give your infant children a comfortable upbringing.

Example will for a married couple with children

The following example is that of a husband, but it could equally well be that of a wife with similar assets. Notes regarding its content follow on pages 67-9.

This will dated [day, month, year] is made by me [full name] of [address].

1 I revoke all earlier wills and codicils.

2 a I appoint as my executors and trustees my [wife] [full name] and my [brother] [full name].
   b If my [wife] [name] or my [brother] [name] are unwilling or unable to act or if they die before me I appoint [friend] [name] in their place.

3 If my [wife] [name] dies before me I appoint [name] and [name] to be the guardians of my infant children.

4 I give to [name] my [any chattel] free of all taxes.

5 I give the following legacies free from all taxes:
   a To my [brother] [name] the sum of [amount] if he proves my will.
   b To my [friend] [name] the sum of [amount] if he proves my will.
   c If my [wife] has died before me I leave [amount] to each of my [nephews] and [nieces] who are living at my death.
   d If my [wife] has died before me I give to the [charity] of [address] the sum of [amount] and confirm that the receipt of a person who appears to be a proper officer of the charity shall be a discharge to my trustees.

6 I give the residue of my estate (after payment of my debts, funeral expenses and any Inheritance Tax) as follows:
   a To my [wife] [name] absolutely if she survives me.
   b If she does not survive me to my trustees who shall hold the residue on trust to divide it equally between my children providing they attain 21 but if either of them should die before me leaving children those children shall on attaining 21 take equally between them the share which my deceased child would have taken if he or she had survived me.

7 My trustees shall have the following powers:

    a To pay income to which a beneficiary under 21 is entitled to his parent or guardian for his benefit or to the beneficiary himself upon reaching 16.

    b To apply capital for the benefit of any beneficiary who is under 21 as if the Trustee Act 1925 section 32 applied to the whole (and not just half) of the beneficiary's interest in that capital.

    c If the house of the guardians of my children is too small to accommodate their family and my children my trustees may lend money to the guardians in order to improve the house or to purchase a new house upon terms which in the opinion of the trustees will not cause the guardians to lose money.

8 I wish my body to be cremated and my ashes scattered at a place to be chosen by my executors but I would like it to be accompanied by a nonreligious ceremony, the form of which I leave to my executors although I may leave guidance in the form of a letter.

Signed by [testator's full name] in our presence
and attested by us in his presence and   [signature of testator]
in the presence of each other:

Witness 1: signed
Full name
Address
Occupation

Witness 2: signed
Full name
Address
Occupation

Notes relating to the example will

Generally This text uses a simpler, more straightforward style than a professional service might use. This is in keeping with the emphasis on clarity in home will writing. Solicitors and online services can draw on centuries of experience that are not available to you at home.

Clause 1 Remember that the will takes effect on your death, so you can revoke it at any time before then. It is possible to amend a will by signing a codicil without revoking the will in full (see pages 7–8). When making a will, it is important to revoke any previous will and codicil so that there can be no confusion about the provisions that govern your estate on your death (unless you have made a foreign will to deal with foreign property).

Clause 2 The main beneficiary is appointed to be executor. Quite apart from saying what should happen if that beneficiary does not survive, you could decide to appoint a substitute executor in case either executor is unable or unwilling to deal with the administration of the estate when the time comes. Any executor can renounce the appointment, although no one, not even a spouse or other co-executor, can force another executor to renounce.

Clause 3 This clause appoints guardians but clause 7 makes financial provision for them in case the parents die before their children are grown up.

Clause 4 It may seem far-fetched to allow for taxes arising on a small gift and where IHT is payable, it is usual for this to be paid out of the residue of the estate before the residuary beneficiaries get their share. In fact, the law automatically implies this but a change in the law is always possible. The phrase 'free from all taxes' also avoids complications if you have made sizeable gifts in the seven years immediately prior to death, using up all your nil-rate tax band. Any gift in a will can, however, be made to carry its own tax (which would be a pro-rata share of the total tax payable). It is therefore proper for the will to state whether any gift should be free of tax or that the beneficiary will have to pay the relevant proportion of the tax on the estate.

Remember also that if any of these items is not owned by the testator at the date of death, the beneficiary will not receive that item and the clause in the will becomes void.

Clause 5d In relation to the gift to a charity, the clause providing for the proper discharge of the executors if they get a receipt from an officer at the charity means that the executors cannot be blamed for paying the money to the wrong people. Give the full name and address, as some charities have very similar names.

Clause 6 This deals with the residuary estate: here, all the rest of the property to your spouse. If the estate of your spouse is likely to be liable for IHT on their (second) death, think carefully before you insert a condition that the beneficiary must survive 30 days to inherit. It can have bad consequences if a nil-rate band is not utilised (see page 57). An investment adviser or a solicitor might well advise you to include a nil-rate band discretionary trust (see box, below) in your will as it would give greater flexibility and more scope for tax-avoidance. This will follows the traditional form, which is still appropriate for smaller estates.

Clause 6b This directs what happens to the property if your spouse dies before you. Where there is a gift to children or a gift where it will be necessary to wait to see if it works (does a child reach 21? how many grandchildren will there be?), there will be a trust. The wording of clause 6b creates such a trust by saying that the trustees are to hold the residue on trust.

In a will, there is always a power of sale (even if the words are not actually used) so that the executors can administer the estate properly. They have to have sufficient cash to pay all the taxes, debts and liabilities, so assets must be sold to realise cash. However, so that the executors can keep the particular gifts given by clause 4, for example, and also keep anything they think might be a good investment, they are given a discretion to postpone the sale of anything for as long as they think fit,

provided they raise sufficient cash to pay all the debts and liabilities and taxes. They are also given the power to invest or apply the money as if it were their own. The executors will have to take proper advice as to the investments, not only because it is the sensible thing to do but also because the law says so. The clause does not mean they can help themselves to the cash.

In this example, the children will be entitled to the property when they become 21. However, children become legally entitled to inherit at the age of 18 unless your will says otherwise. If you want to postpone the age at which a child will become entitled to inherit to a greater age than 21, take legal advice as there are a number of taxation complications to watch.

Clause 7 A set of provisions has been prepared by the Society of Trust and Estate Practioners (STEP). If you wish, clause 7 could read 'The Standard Provisions of the Society for Trust and Estate Practitioners (1st edition) shall apply.' For details of these provisions and their application, see the box, below).

Clauses 7a and b Where infant children are entitled to property under a trust such as this, the law automatically imposes provisions (by virtue of Sections 31 and 32 of the Trustee Act 1925)

For details of the Society of Trust and Estate Practitioners (STEP) provisions and their application, see www.step.org. The provisions shown in the spcimen will are intended as examples of what can be written into a will.

that allow the trustees to use any part of the income for the children's benefit and up to one-half of the capital to which they will become entitled on attaining the given age. The children might miss an opportunity if their trustees were to be restricted to using only one-half of the children's interest for their benefit. For instance, the children might be showing a particular aptitude for some profession or activity and require more capital than one-half of their prospective interest to be trained in that profession. Such a provision is particularly relevant where children do not become entitled until the age of 21, or even older. The provisions of the Trustee Act have therefore been widened in this will by saying that any part of the capital (not just up to one-half) could be so used.

Clause 7c Even if the guardians are the same people as the trustees, they have to keep separate the two different functions. They should keep proper accounts of all financial payments, receipts and transactions. In this example,

the testator has realised that the guardians might require a larger house, but he does not want to make an outright payment shortly before his children reach 18 because then the children might have more need of money for themselves. It is important to be clear what payment (if any) will be made to the guardians from the estate so that they are not out of pocket, but it is equally important not to waste capital on them, especially if the children are nearly independent when their parents die. Take great care when deciding whether (and, if so, how) guardians should be paid.

Clause 8 Use whatever wording you choose to describe the sort of funeral you would like.

❝ Be clear about what payment (if any) will be made to the guardians from the estate. ❞

Executors' and trustees' powers of investment

This is now largely governed by the provisions of the Trustee Act 2000. This Act describes the duty of care that a trustee must exercise together with his or her powers of investment, his or her power to employ agents and his or her right to recover expenses and, in certain cases, the trustees' right to remuneration. The provisions set out in a will may enlarge the powers and extend the rights of trustees, but in all cases the trustees must normally obtain and consider proper advice when making or reviewing the investments of their trust.

WILL OF A HUSBAND/ WIFE/CIVIL PARTNER WITH GROWN-UP CHILDREN

Where there are adult children and the total family assets are below £600,000, you need to think about how and when to benefit your children. Ask yourself:

- **Does it make sense to make a lifetime gift to your children?**
- **Do you need to establish a discretionary trust** so that money is not lost to bankrupt or divorcing children, or a surviving spouse or civil partner ending his or her days in a nursing home?

If you have made substantial gifts within the last seven years, you could consider leaving your spouse or civil partner a specific sum of money or property that will not be taxed, even if that would dispose of most of your estate. The remainder – your residuary estate out of which IHT will be paid – could then pass to your children. The will could take a similar form to the example on pages 65–6, with an additional clause as follows:

New clause 6 To my [wife] [name] I give the sum of £150,000 and all my interest in property known as [address], or any other property which is our main residence at the date of my death.

New clause 7 I give the rest of my estate to my trustees on trust for sale as follows:

  a To pay my debts and testamentary expenses as well as any Inheritance Tax on my estate.

  b To divide what is left equally between my children [name] and [name] but if either should die before me leaving children, those children should take equally the share which their deceased parent would otherwise have inherited.

Old clauses 7 and 8 would then be re-numbered as 8 and 9.

If your joint estates are worth more than £600,000 you may hit a problem if you make a large, tax-free bequest to, say, a daughter and then give what is left to your spouse or civil partner (who is exempt from IHT). The law states that the value of the tax-free gift must then be 'grossed up' to include the tax payable as well as the gift. Seek advice if this looks likely.

If there have been no gifts during the last seven years, and provided you are happy that your spouse or civil partner would have sufficient finances to maintain him or her for the rest of his or her life, then it may make sense to give legacies to the value of the nil-rate band before leaving the residue to your spouse or civil partner.

Your spouse or civil partner would do the same, although it might be necessary to equalise your estates in order to make the most of this action. The legacies to be given, which could therefore total up to £600,000, need not necessarily be given to your children but could be given to any beneficiary other than your spouse or civil partner (for whom all your gifts are tax exempt). It is uncommon to create a nil-rate band discretionary trust by the will, which can then be used to distribute that money to a variety of beneficiaries (see page 35).

WILL OF A SINGLE PERSON

Your will can be quite short. You just need to think about the appointment of executors, a few legacies perhaps and then the disposal of the residue to one or more people, including substitute beneficiaries in case any of your beneficiaries die before you. The administrative provisions can be taken care of by reference to the Standard Provisions of the Society of Trust and Estate Practitioners (STEP) (see page 68).

If you are an elderly person who is single, divorced or widowed, it is best to choose executors who can arrange your funeral and also secure your house at short notice, especially if you have no close relatives.

❝ If, after drawing up your will, you get married to the main beneficiary of your estate, remember that this will then revoke your will. ❞

WILL OF AN UNMARRIED COUPLE WITH NO CHILDREN

If you and your partner are not intending to get married, you should make your wills as soon as possible in the usual way. Remember, there is no IHT exemption for transfers of IHT allowance between cohabiting couples. Other benefits, such as widow's pension, will also not be available.

If, after drawing up your will, you do get married, remember that a will is usually revoked on marriage. To avoid this problem, insert a special non-revocation clause at the beginning of your respective wills, which might read as follows:

1 This will shall not be revoked by my intended marriage to [partner's name].

If no time limit is inserted, the will remains valid even if the relationship breaks up.

If you want your wills to take effect only on your wedding, then the clause could read:

1 This will is made in contemplation of and is conditional upon my marriage to [partner's name].

In the latter case, however, bear in mind that until the wedding, you will be

The Society of Trust and Estate Practitioners (STEP) is an organisation aimed at furthering the knowledge and expertise of specialists in trust and estate management. To find out more, go to www.step.org.

intestate. It is therefore much better to use the first alternative unless there is some special reason for the latter (see also page 81).

Reversion of property

For unmarried couples, you may want your property to revert to your own family rather than go to the family of your partner or perhaps to the family of someone else whom the survivor may marry or live with in the future, and who would then benefit through your partner's will.

There are a number of ways of dealing with this. Bear in mind that it cannot be known in advance which partner will die first, nor the period of time between the two deaths. It may be five minutes, five days or 50 years. Some couples feel that, provided it is likely that the survivor will have a long life after the death of the first person to die, then it is right and proper for the survivor to benefit absolutely from all the property. To make sure, the survivorship period may be extended to three or even six months in the case of some common accident, so that the property will pass to the survivor unless the deaths are close together.

One way in which you can be certain that your property will revert to your own family on the death of your partner is to limit the benefit of your partner to a 'life interest only' (see pages 51–2), allowing your partner the use of the property for her or his life and then dictating who benefits from that property on the death of your partner, for example, your own family. This, however, requires the creation of a trust, so it would be sensible to take legal advice.

WILL OF A DIVORCED/ SEPARATED PERSON

If you wish to avoid any benefit going to a previous or separated spouse or civil partner, seek legal advice because there can be complications; your former spouse or civil partner might make an application to the court for a share in your estate regardless of the terms of the will, particularly if the division of the matrimonial property has not been finalised or if you were still paying maintenance at the time of your death.

Show your adviser any order of the divorce court dealing with matrimonial assets or maintenance. Clean-break divorce settlements usually preclude the parties from claiming against one another's estates, but the situation is different if there is a continuing obligation to pay maintenance.

If you have a new partner who you wish to benefit for the rest of his or her life, but then want the property to go back to your children by a first marriage, it would be necessary to create a trust giving a life interest to the new partner, who would live in the property and/or enjoy the income for the rest of his or her life. After your partner's death the property would revert to your children (see pages 51–2).

Writing your will yourself

If you want to write your own will, it is, of course, perfectly possible to do so, but do judge your abilities realistically. Ask yourself why you are not using a reputable online service. Do not take chances with such an important document (see pages 13-16).

WHEN WRITING YOUR OWN WILL

Here are some pointers to help you:

- **Write your will in draft form first,** and amend as necessary to tidy up the wording. Traditionally, lawyers did not use punctuation in legal documents but, if used as an aid towards clarity, there is no reason why a will should not be punctuated.

- **Type out the will.** It can be written by hand, but typing is better to make it is legible. Use single line spacing, so that it fits on to two sides of one sheet of paper, leaving sufficient room at the end for your signature and those of your witnesses, together with their printed names, addresses and occupations.

- **If you make any mistakes,** rectify them before printing out a clean copy. Any alterations appearing in the will are assumed – unless the contrary is proved – to have been made after the will was signed, and so form no part of it.

- **if a will extends to more than one sheet of paper,** it is best to leave one full clause for the next page to make any tampering with your will as difficult as possible. Also, if the continuation is

on a fresh sheet, you and your witnesses should sign at the bottom of the first sheet.

- **Make sure that each page** of your will is numbered so that no one can craftily slip in a couple of extra pages containing benefits to him- or herself.

- **Do not leave blank the back page** of any sheet of paper on which your will is written. Either continue with the clauses on to the back of each page, or draw a line right across the blank space and put your initials at the top and bottom of the line. Ask your witnesses to do the same. The aim is to make any tampering with your will as difficult as possible and to make it obvious which are the sheets of paper that comprise your will, each sheet of which should bear your signature and the signatures of your witnesses at the bottom.

USING AN ONLINE SERVICE TO WRITE YOUR WILL

If you decide to use an online service, you will need to think about the things that are dealt with in this book (see the checklist on pages 62-3). The service cannot think for you, so you should need to think about the things in this book before you start. Use the points below to help you use an online service for the best result:

- **With a good service** it will be possible to save your work and return to it another time; for example, you may have forgotten someone's middle name or address and need to enquire. Nevertheless, it is a good thing if you are prepared and have all the information assembled before you start.
- **The service should be efficient** but speed is not necessarily a good thing. Making a will is an important action, and should be done with care, and deliberately.
- **The service should filter out your case** if it is not suitable for you. It is still probably a good idea for you to work out for yourself if you are not a candidate to use an online service at all. Be honest with yourself. It is not worth saving a few hundred pounds if you are going to get it wrong – whatever you spend is wasted if the result is not right.
- **You should spend** between one and three hours on preparing, using the service, reading over the will, signing it, storing and copying it. The time will not be spent in one continuous session but over a number of stages.

You should not be using an online service if:

- **You have any sort of foreign connection.** This means that you should not be using

one if England or Wales is not your permanent home. You should also not be using an online service if you think that England or Wales might not be the permanent home of your spouse or civil partner. (If you are in Scotland or Northern Ireland, you can use an online service that is intended for people who permanently live in those parts of the country, but with the same qualifications: do not use the service if you are in doubt about where your permanent home is or about whether your spouse or civil partner has one in the same place). You should probably also not be using an online service if you own property abroad
- **Your family circumstances are complicated** by having more than one family.
- **You are very substantially wealthy,** or have a farm or farm property, or have a business of your own. Nor should you be using it if there are family trusts in which you are involved.

You certainly should not try to 'beat' the system in the online service. For example, the Which? system filters you out if you co-own property with someone, but do not wish for your co-owner to inherit it. Do not start again and try to cheat the system by inputting that you do not have such property. The filter is there for a reason (for more on jointly-owned property, see pages 23 and 111-12).

To obtain your exclusive £10 discount for the Which? Wills service, start writing your will at www.whichwills.com and use the voucher code WH-WANDP at payment stage. For more, see page 208. The closing date of the offer is 30 June 2011.

Making alterations to a will

There may be a change of circumstance in your life that prompts you to alter your will. For small amendments, use a codicil; for anything major, it is best to write a new will. After your death, it might be advantageous for your beneficiaries to amend or vary your will, which is done by a deed of variation. This chapter explains in what circumstances this might be necessary.

Changing a will

If you have made a will, you can change it at any time. It is particularly important that you should review it whenever circumstances change and, in any event, every five years as legislation can change, even if personal circumstances do not. If you do change your will, you should take personal responsibility for destroying your previous will together with any copies of it.

If you change your will, you must not cross out parts of it, or write bits in, or make any alterations whatsoever on it. The will is valid in the form in which it stood on the day it was signed. Any obvious alterations made on the face of a will are presumed – until the contrary is proved – to have been made after the original signing and witnessing took place and so do not form part of the legally valid will. Furthermore, any legacy that appears underneath your signature is not valid.

In theory, you could make subsequent alterations on the will itself by signing the altered will and having that new signature witnessed again, as was done when the will was first signed. But this is messy and unsatisfactory, and quite the wrong way to go about making alterations to a will. Either write a codicil or start again.

❝ Deleting part of a will can render it invalid. ❞

When you might want to change your will

- You are getting married.
- The birth of your first child.
- You are going through a divorce.
- You are getting married for a second time.
- The death of a partner.
- For tax reasons, perhaps because you have just made a very large gift (and there is, of course, no guarantee that you will live another seven years – see pages 30-1), or because seven years have elapsed since you made any large gifts, or because there have been changes in tax law.
- A change of heart following a difference of opinion.

CODICILS

If all you want to do is make a simple alteration to your will, either by revoking a provision or by adding something, you could do this by making a codicil. This is really nothing more than a supplement to a will, which makes some alteration to it but leaves the rest of it standing. You might want to make a codicil to:

- **Increase a cash legacy** to take account of inflation since you made the will.
- **Re-allocate a bequest** because the intended recipient has died.
- **Change the executors or guardians** – the guardians you have chosen may have become separated or divorced, or they may now not wish to be your executors. A codicil can include a provision revoking the appointment and substituting others.

- **Specify that a will previously made** should be 'in anticipation of marriage' (see page 71). In this way, the marriage will not revoke the will.

There is no limit on how many codicils you may make. Some people make quite a few, but a codicil is suitable only for a straightforward alteration to a will. For anything more than that, it is better to make a completely new will anyway and not bother making a codicil.

It is advisable to number codicils so that the executors know they have them all. If a testator has moved around, he or she may have a will at a solicitor's; the first codicil at his or her mother's house; a second codicil in a box under the bed and the third codicil at the bank. If they are not numbered, the executors could miss one or more without realising it.

I, [name] of [address] declare this to be a first codicil to my will dated [day] [month] [year].

1 I revoke the bequest of my [chattels] to my [brother] [name].
2 I give [amount] to my [brother] [name].
3 In all other respects I confirm my will.
Date: [day] [month] [year]

Signed by [testator's full name] in our presence and attested by us in his presence and in the presence of each other: [signature of testator]

Witness 1: signed   Witness 2: signed
Full name   Full name
Address   Address
Occupation   Occupation

To be valid, a codicil must be signed and witnessed in exactly the same way as a will. It has to be signed by the testator in the presence of two witnesses and they must both sign it in the presence of the testator (see pages 59–60). The witnesses do not have to be the same who witnessed the original will. Here is an example:

Provided it contains a clause in the terms of clause 3 in the example on page 77, a codicil acts as a confirmation of everything contained in the will that has not been expressly revoked by it,

and the will has to be construed as at the date of the codicil. To find out the whole of the testator's wishes, both the will and the codicil have to be considered.

DEED OF VARIATION

The provisions of a will or the rules of distribution on an intestacy can be varied after the death and, provided certain conditions are observed, the variations will be accepted as though they had been set out in the original will or intestacy.

The executors should be looking for the tax benefits that could result from a post-death variation, but if a beneficiary thinks that tax could be reduced in this way, he should bring it to the attention of the executors straight away. A typical example might arise, as shown in the case study, below.

A deed of variation is an extremely useful document, which can save large

> **❝ A deed of variation can be implemented where there are tax benefits to be had and provided certain conditions are met. ❞**

Case Study **Mr and Mrs Howe**

Mr Howe died in May 2009, leaving £200,000, of which £50,000 is left to his children and the balance of £150,000 goes to his long-term partner, Ms Rodney, who had £300,000 of her own. No IHT is payable.

Then, in July 2009, Ms Rodney died, leaving all of the £450,000 to their children. Tax of £50,000 is payable. The overall result is that the children have £450,000. As two years hadn't elapsed

since Mr Howe died, a deed of variation could be drawn up so that the amount left to the children in Mr Howe's will could rise from £50,000 to £200,000.

There will still be no tax to pay in Mr Howe's estate, but the amount passing to Ms Rodney will be reduced from £150,000 to £0 so her own estate will only be £300,000. There will then be no tax to pay in her estate either. Their children will be better off by £50,000.

sums of IHT, although the merging of IHT allowances for married couples and civil partners means it is no longer as useful for making use of the nil-rate band in both estates as has been the case in the past.

However, if you are administering an estate on which IHT is payable, you should consider whether a deed of variation could be used to reduce tax. It can even be used to change a joint tenancy of a house into a tenancy in common (see box, below) or to renounce a legacy. A rewritten will can also be used to bypass a generation by transferring assets from grandparents to grandchildren, thus saving IHT on the estate of grown-up children.

The following conditions apply to any deed of variation:

- The variation must be in writing.
- The variation must be made within two years of the death.
- The beneficiaries must agree (if the beneficiaries are under 18 or subject to a Court of Protection order, consent will have to be obtained from a court if the deed is to be made on their behalf).
- The executors' agreement must be obtained if the variation results in more IHT becoming payable.

If a variation of a deceased spouse or civil partner's will is being considered during the lifetime of the surviving spouse or civil partner, it is important to make sure that the surviving person retains enough capital for the rest of his or her life and to support any children while they are still young.

The recent merging of individual IHT thresholds into one allowance of £600,000 for married couples and civil partners may cause some people to expect that intestacy rules have also been amended to match. They have not. A post-death deed of variation may help some families to replace the intestacy rules with a sensible will.

❝ Despite the merging of individual IHT thresholds into one allowance of £600,000 for married couples and civil partners, intestacy rules have not been amended to match. ❞

See page 23 for definitions of a joint tenancy and a tenancy in common together with information on how one form of tenancy can be more beneficial than another, depending on the circumstances.

Revoking a will

If you make a will, it should normally contain a clause that revokes any previous will and codicil. There are, however, other ways of revoking a will apart from including a specific clause of this sort – destroying it or getting married.

REVOKING BY DESTRUCTION

If you deliberately burn, tear up or in some other way destroy your will, it is revoked. It must be a deliberate act. If your will were to be accidentally burned, whether by you or by someone else, it would not be revoked. There have, in fact, been cases where a will has been declared valid after the testator's death, the original having been accidentally destroyed. In one case, for instance, the torn-up pieces were assembled and proved as a valid will when it was shown that it was torn up in mistake for an old letter.

In order for a will to be effectively revoked, it is the testator who must burn it or tear it up. Alternatively, this may be done by someone at the testator's direction. However it is done, the testator has to be present or the will is not revoked. For example, the will would

not properly be revoked if the testator were to write to the bank manager who kept it, telling him or her to destroy it, even if the manager did so. (There will be serious problems to overcome if no one knows for sure what was in a will that has been destroyed but had not been revoked.)

“A will is revoked where a will is destroyed by being deliberately burned or torn up. If a will were accidentally burned, it would not be revoked. ”

 The revocation clause is a standard phrase (see page 65) that should be used in all wills. Page 56 explains why it is necessary.

REVOKING BY MARRIAGE

The other way of revoking a will is surprising and is not always remembered: getting married. The law supposes that a man or a woman who has made a will and later gets married does not want that will to stand. As a result, merely to get married without saying anything about an existing will revokes the will. The whole will is revoked, including any legacies to people wholly independent of the new husband or wife.

This can lead to some curious results. Imagine that a widow with young children has made a will leaving her property to the children. Some years later she marries again. She must make a new will just before the marriage and with a clause stating that it is in anticipation of marriage to the second husband, otherwise, when she dies, her death will be intestate and her second husband would inherit the first £125,000 of her estate (see page 141) with her children getting a share of what was left, if anything. If she waits until after the marriage to make a new will, it is possible she could die just after the marriage and before making a new will.

Another unusual situation could arise if a long-established cohabiting couple (who have made wills) get married. Their wills would immediately become void (see page 71).

Not always revoked by marriage

It is, however, possible to make a will (or add a codicil, see page 77), which says that it is made in contemplation of a forthcoming marriage. The will must state that it is made in contemplation of marriage to a particular person, who must be named, and also that the testator intends that the will shall not be revoked by his or her marriage to that person.

Such a will is then not revoked by that marriage but, should that marriage not happen and, instead, the testator marries someone else, the will is then revoked. If no marriage whatever takes place, the will, of course, remains effective – unless it was made conditional on the particular contemplated marriage taking place within a certain period of time.

❝ The other way to revoke a will is by getting married. The whole will is revoked, including any legacies to people independent of the new husband or wife. ❞

 For an idea of the correct wording to use in a will or codicil in anticipation of a marriage, see 'Will of an unmarried couple with no children' on page 71.

THE EFFECT OF DIVORCE

Divorce does not automatically revoke all the provisions of a will. The effect of divorce is that any appointment of the former spouse as an executor will be invalid, and any gift in the will to the former spouse will be treated as if the former spouse had died on the date of the divorce. Where the gift is a specific one – for example, of a house or £10,000 – such property will go to whoever is entitled to the residue of the estate. But where, under the terms of the will, the former spouse was given the residue of the estate without further provision, it will instead be dealt with in accordance with the intestacy rules. The same will apply to a civil partner.

If you are contemplating divorce, it is possible to cover this situation by executing a short codicil before the decree is pronounced, amending the circumstances in which the children will benefit to include the divorce. This would read along the lines of:

'In clause [x] of my will after the words "does not survive me for the period of thirty days" shall be inserted the words "or we are divorced at the time of my death"'.

Following a divorce, it is then best to make a new will.

> **The effect of divorce is that any appointment of the former spouse as an executor will become invalid.**

Storing your will

It may seem obvious, but it is a wise precaution to let at least your executors know where they can find your will after you have died. There are a few options, which are covered in this chapter.

Where to keep your will

From the moment your will is signed and witnessed and dated, it is valid. There is no law requiring that wills must be registered before death. Instead, it is up to you to find a safe place for the will, to put it there and to let your executors know where it is. Don't forget to tell your executors if you move it or destroy it.

The main thing about storing your will, is to keep it somewhere safe.

- **If your will has been prepared by a solicitor,** the original will usually be kept in the solicitor's strong room (free of charge) and you will be given a copy.
- **If your will is kept in a bank deposit box,** you will have to pay an annual fee. It may also be helpful to make the executor known to the bank.
- **If you keep it in your own safe at home,** make sure that the whereabouts of the key or the combination is known to someone else or your executors will have to call a safebreaker before they can apply for probate.

Quite a few people lodge their wills in their bank but you will be charged for the service and it may take time to obtain the release of the will following death. If you decide to keep your will at home, perhaps the best place to keep it is wherever you keep your other important documents – marriage and birth certificates, savings certificates, title deeds of the house, and so on. Put the will in an envelope and seal it, and write on the outside your full name, the word 'WILL' in large letters and the date. No further formalities are required before putting the will safely away. However, wills have been known to disappear when kept at home, so beware.

> **❝Wills have been known to disappear when kept at home, so beware.❞**

 You can find out more about storing wills at the Principal Probate Registery at www.hmcourts-service.gov.uk/cms/1202.htm.

Information for next-of-kin and executors upon your death

Write down all this information in one place and then hand it to your next-of-kin and/or executors – or tell them where to find it – so that everyone knows your intentions in the event of your death.

Personal information

Your name, address, postcode and telephone number

Where your will and other important papers are located

Their location and the date of your latest will (perhaps with a copy of your will)

Medical information

Your NHS number, location of medical card and doctor's name, address and telephone number

Before the funeral

Give the details (name, address, telephone number) of the person(s) who you would like to make the funeral arrangements, such as registering the death and contacting the funeral director, although this will usually be the executor.

People to contact following your death

Give the details (name, address, telephone number) of:

- Relatives and friends
- Your solicitor
- Your employer
- Financial contacts (bank, building society) + account type and number
- Accountant
- Tax adviser
- Insurance companies/broker

Funeral instructions

Any specific instructions about leaving your body for medical research or for transplants that aren't included in your will (see also page 55).

If you have a pre-paid funeral plan, a particular grave reserved or know which funeral director you would like to be used, write down the details.

KEEPING UP TO DATE

As time goes by and your situation develops and changes, you should keep your list of assets and liabilities up to date (as well as your will). Your objective should be to make things as easy as possible for your executors and family when you die. Any tendency to be secretive about your assets is likely to make life more difficult for your executors unless there is comprehensive information with your will. You should also keep your list up to date as to where the essential documents are to be found (see the checklist on the previous page).

**“** By keeping your will in a safe, accessible place and ensuring all related paperwork is well organised, you will make your executors' duties so much easier. **”**

STORING DOCUMENTS

The logical course, obviously, is to keep things such as share certificates, building society accounts books, savings certificates, insurance policies, title deeds and all similar documents in one place – a family safe, for instance, or a locked drawer (make sure that someone knows where the keys are). This may be the same place where you keep your will. If you keep your affairs tidy and orderly, so far as possible, when the time comes for your executors to act, they will not find that they have taken on an investigation instead of an administration.

If you want to, you can deposit your will at the Principal Probate Registry (see box at foot of page 84). If you write to the record-keeper at the Principal Registry, you will be sent a large envelope and instructions about completing all the details requested on it, signing and witnessing, and where it should be taken or sent. A small fee is payable. You will be given a deposit certificate, which has to be produced if the will is to be withdrawn. The Administration of Justice Act 1982 may eventually establish a new system for the deposit and registration of wills.

There is no special advantage in depositing a will in this formal manner (rather than, say, putting it in a safe or depositing it with your bank). For example, it does not prevent future wills or codicils being made.

Applying for probate

Up to this point, this book has been concerned with creating your own will. Now, however, we turn to obtaining probate for someone else's estate, which includes fulfilling the terms of someone else's will. The chapter assumes that you are either an executor or administrator.

Administering an estate

On someone's death, their estate is administered by an executor or administrator. An **executor** is the person responsible for administering an estate, and will have been named in the deceased's will; an **administrator** does the same job as an executor but is appointed because the deceased died intestate – that is, without leaving a will – or failed to include the names of executors in his or her will.

EXECUTOR OR ADMINISTRATOR?

When someone makes a will you should have been asked if he or she wanted you to be one of the executors. Hopefully, you will also have been informed as to the whereabouts of the will or at least be able to find it relatively easily. On the death of that person, you, as executor, will become responsible for administering the estate and applying for probate.

The term 'probate' (or 'probate of the will') means a legal document issued to one or more people ('the executors') by the Probate Registry authorising them to deal with an estate. The Probate Registry must grant probate, known as the grant of representation, but can only do so after seeing legal proof that you are the executor. Once granted, the grant of representation proves that you are entitled to claim the assets of the deceased, not for yourself but in your capacity as personal representative. You are then in a position to administer the estate and must follow the will and deal with the estate and beneficiaries according to the law.

When someone dies without leaving a will (and recent research shows this could be as many as half the population), the rules of intestacy then come into play and this is when you might discover that you are designated to be the administrator for that person's estate. The nearest relatives, in a fixed order (see page 11), are entitled to apply for

❝An executor is appointed by a will; an administrator is appointed when someone dies intestate. Their duties are the same.❞

the grant – known in this instance as the 'letters of administration'. If the nearest relative does not wish to apply, he or she can renounce his or her right to do so, in which case the next-nearest relative becomes entitled to be the administrator, and so on, down the line of kinship as set out in the list on page 11. If there are no relatives willing to do the job, the application can be made by the Treasury Solicitor on behalf of the Crown or by a creditor of the deceased.

If you are the next of kin responsible for administering an intestate estate, you will have to apply to the Probate Registry for the letters of administration, which confirms that you are able to administer the estate of the deceased relative. The procedure is the same as that adopted by executors applying for a grant of probate.

If a will does not name an executor or if the executors are unable or unwilling to apply for the grant of probate, the person entitled to apply for letters of administration makes the application to the registrar in the same way, but the grant of representation is then known as letters of administration with will annexed.

The flow chart overleaf sets out the essential steps of applying for probate of the will.

> **!** An important distinction between probate and letters of administration is that administrators have no legal authority to act until the grant of letters of administration is issued to them, whereas executors may act immediately on the death.

❝ The letters of administration confirm that you are able to administer the estate of your deceased relative. ❞

The Principal Probate Registry is your first point of contact. Either phone the helpline 0845 302 0900 or go to website www.hmrc.gov.uk/inheritancetax and follow the links to probate. From here you will find links to all relevant websites. The form PA2 – 'How to obtain probate', which is available from www.hmcourts-service.gov.uk – is a useful guide to get hold of immediately.

Applying for probate: the procedure

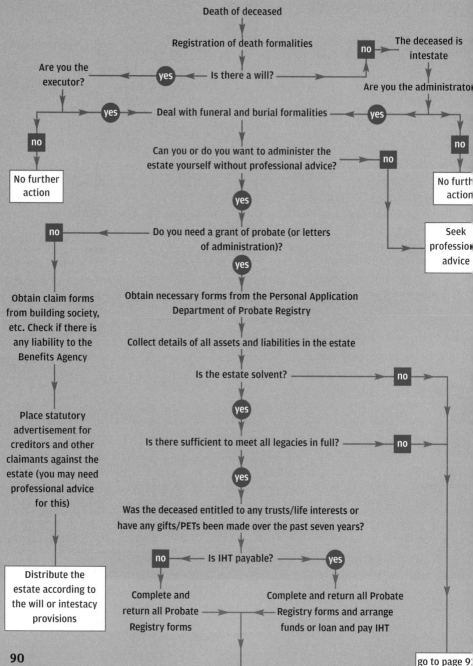

Death of deceased

Registration of death formalities

Is there a will? — **no** → The deceased is intestate

yes → Are you the executor?

Are you the administrator?

Are you the executor? **yes** → Deal with funeral and burial formalities ← **yes** — Are you the administrator?

no → No further action

no → No further action

Can you or do you want to administer the estate yourself without professional advice? → **no**

yes

no ← Do you need a grant of probate (or letters of administration)? → Seek professional advice

yes

Obtain claim forms from building society, etc. Check if there is any liability to the Benefits Agency

Obtain necessary forms from the Personal Application Department of Probate Registry

Collect details of all assets and liabilities in the estate

Is the estate solvent? → **no** →

yes

Place statutory advertisement for creditors and other claimants against the estate (you may need professional advice for this)

Is there sufficient to meet all legacies in full? → **no** →

yes

Was the deceased entitled to any trusts/life interests or have any gifts/PETs been made over the past seven years?

no ← Is IHT payable? → **yes**

Distribute the estate according to the will or intestacy provisions

Complete and return all Probate Registry forms

Complete and return all Probate Registry forms and arrange funds or loan and pay IHT

90

go to page 91

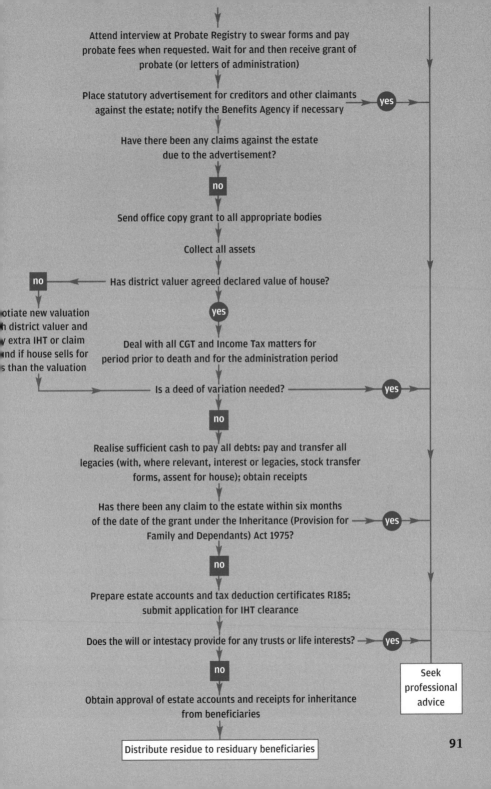

Attend interview at Probate Registry to swear forms and pay probate fees when requested. Wait for and then receive grant of probate (or letters of administration)

Place statutory advertisement for creditors and other claimants against the estate; notify the Benefits Agency if necessary → **yes** →

Have there been any claims against the estate due to the advertisement?

no

Send office copy grant to all appropriate bodies

Collect all assets

no ← Has district valuer agreed declared value of house?

otiate new valuation
h district valuer and
y extra IHT or claim
nd if house sells for
s than the valuation

yes

Deal with all CGT and Income Tax matters for period prior to death and for the administration period

→ Is a deed of variation needed? → **yes** →

no

Realise sufficient cash to pay all debts: pay and transfer all legacies (with, where relevant, interest or legacies, stock transfer forms, assent for house); obtain receipts

Has there been any claim to the estate within six months of the date of the grant under the Inheritance (Provision for Family and Dependants) Act 1975? → **yes** →

no

Prepare estate accounts and tax deduction certificates R185; submit application for IHT clearance

Does the will or intestacy provide for any trusts or life interests? → **yes** →

no

Obtain approval of estate accounts and receipts for inheritance from beneficiaries

Distribute residue to residuary beneficiaries

Seek professional advice

91

OBTAINING A WILL

The most usual place to keep a homemade will is somewhere at home (see page 84), but wilful or accidental destruction could have serious consequences, so many testators choose to keep their will in their bank or with their solicitor.

If the will is lodged in the bank, you, as executor, will have to sign for it or acknowledge its safe receipt in writing

if it is sent by post. Where several executors are named in the will, the bank should ask for all their signatures before releasing the will to one of them.

Sometimes the will may be held in a solicitor's office safe. There should be no need for the solicitor to keep the will, and he or she should release it to you against your and any other executor's signatures. If the solicitor is also one of the executors, he or she will expect to be involved in the administration, but if the firm is to deal with the administration of the estate, make sure you are clear about the basis on which the firm will charge (see pages 100–1). If the solicitor who was appointed an executor has left the firm concerned, or has retired, he or she must be contacted. He or she may be prepared to renounce as executor (but you can't force an executor to do this; see box, below), leaving you free to administer the estate without having to use a particular firm of solicitors.

The reading of a will

A formal reading of the will to the family after the funeral is a ritual that now happens mostly (though not entirely) in the world of fiction. It is usual for the executor or administrator to inform the beneficiaries of the contents of the will at an early stage although you should remember that anyone can see a copy once probate has been obtained.

There is always a slight risk that the will might be found invalid for some reason (see pages 38–41), or that a later will might be found, or that there is not enough in the estate to pay out all the legacies. So although it is a good idea to inform beneficiaries of the contents of the will to help prevent them from becoming upset or suspicious, ensure they know that no legacy can be positively confirmed until after probate is granted and the estate administered.

> **❝ The most usual place for a homemade will to be kept is at home, but it can also be kept at a bank, solicitor's office or the Principal Probate Registry. ❞**

 Under certain circumstances, an executor can step down from the job – see pages 95–6. Although it isn't possible to force an executor to renounce his or her duties, it is possible to 'encourage' him or her to do so if absolutely necessary: see box on page 42.

Missing wills

If you are in any doubt that the first will to be found is not the last will made by the testator, you will need to undertake a thorough search of any possible place where the previous will could be stored (see page 147).

Copy wills present another problem if the original cannot be found. Did the testator destroy the original on purpose but forget to destroy the copy? Or was the original lost or accidentally destroyed, in which case it may be possible to obtain probate based on the copy? Evidence of the surrounding circumstances will be crucial.

DO I NEED TO APPLY FOR PROBATE?

If all the property of the deceased passes automatically to a beneficiary, e.g. where property is held on a joint tenancy, probate may not be necessary. It is, however, normally required if the value of the estate exceeds £5,000, but the provisions of the Administration of Estates (Small Payments) Act 1965 allows some small estates to be administered without obtaining probate.

Probate will be required in order to sell or transfer any property held only in the name of the deceased or as tenants in common. It isn't needed if the only asset is a house held jointly as beneficial joint

❝If an estate exceeds £5,000, it is necessary to obtain probate. ❞

! If a recent will turns up halfway through the process, a fresh application for probate will have to be made and steps will have to be taken to unscramble any distribution that has already been made.

Accounting to HMRC

Even where probate is not required, HMRC rules demand an account of all property in the estate. However, normally you deliver to the Probate Office only a simplified account (on form IHT205) if the value of the estate is low (no more than £325,000, or exempt (the estate is valued at no more than £1 million but there is no tax to pay because of bequests to a surviving spouse or civil partner or charity).

To find out more about IHT, see pages 29–34, which include information on the seven-year rule and lifetime gifts.

tenants. A house or flat could be advertised for sale soon after the death of the owner, but contracts should not be exchanged before the granting of probate.

An executor who distributes the assets of an estate without obtaining probate might miss the obligation to submit an account to HM Revenue & Customs (HMRC) for Inheritance Tax (IHT) purposes, especially where a substantial gift had been made in the seven years prior to the death or for a longer period if there had been a reservation of interest (see pages 31–2). A failure to declare such gifts could result in serious consequences for the executor.

Jargon buster

Administration of the estate The task of the executor or administrator

Administrator The name given to a personal representative if not appointed by a valid will. The administrator will usually have to obtain letters of administration to show that he or she is the person with legal authority to deal with the property of the deceased

CGT Capital Gains Tax

Executor The name given to a personal representative if he or she is appointed by a valid will or codicil. The executor will usually have to apply for probate of the will to show that he or she is the person with legal authority to deal with the property of the deceased

Grant of probate The document issued by the probate registry to the executors of a will to authorise them to administer the estate

IHT Inheritance Tax

Letters of administration The document issued by the probate registry to administer the estate of an intestate person

Letters of administration with will annexed The document issued by the probate registry to the administrator when there is a will but the will does not deal with everything, e.g. it fails to appoint an executor

Personal representatives A general term for both administrators and executors

Residue Everything that is left once all debts, liabilities, taxes, costs and legacies have been paid

Solvent Value of the assets exceeds any debts and liabilities

 Who can apply for letters of administration? See page 11 for a list setting out in detail the order of those entitled to apply for letters of administration.

DO I NEED TO APPLY FOR LETTERS OF ADMINISTRATION?

As an administrator, you have to apply for letters of administration for exactly the same reasons as an executor has to apply for probate. You may run into difficulties if someone else in the family is equally entitled to apply for letters of administration and you cannot agree who should apply. It could also make it hard to decide who will arrange the funeral and who will take charge of the house. Generally speaking, the grant is made to the first applicant but, in the case of a dispute between equally entitled administrators, consult the Registrar of the Probate Registry.

❝ If you do not want to take part in the administration of a friend or relative's estate, you can renounce probate by filling in a form. ❞

EXECUTORS NOT WILLING TO ACT

There are a number of reasons why someone might not want to be an executor: for instance, a relative or friend who had had no contact with the testator for a long period, or someone who simply does not want to be troubled with the chore and responsibilities of the administration.

If you have no wish to take part in the administration, you can renounce probate (obtain a form of renunciation from OyezStraker, see box below). Alternatively, you can take a back seat but remain a potential executor by allowing your fellow executor(s) to apply for probate with 'power reserved' to you. To do this they must serve notice on you (obtain a power reserved letter from the Probate Registry).

If one of the executors renounces, the substitute (if one is named in the will) automatically comes in, unless he or she also renounces.

It is possible for a person named as executor in the will to appoint an attorney for the purpose of obtaining the grant; the attorney then acts as if he or she had actually been named as the executor in the will. (The appropriate form for this can also be obtained from the Oyez shops.) The attorney can also act for the executor during the rest of

To contact OyezStraker, go to website www.oyezformslink.co.uk, and for the Probate Office, go to www.hmcourts-service.gov.uk. In Northern Ireland you will need to contact the Probate and Matrimonial Office: www.courtsni.gov.uk.

the administration. Usually the power lasts for one year and relieves a personal representative of the form-signing part of the administration. It can be useful where the executor is abroad or infirm.

There are also rules enabling an attorney to act during the incapacity of another and, in some cases, this can cover the incapacity of an executor. The rules are complicated, and, if any question of incapacity through old age or mental illness arises, you should check with the Probate Registry.

&& Arrangements are in place at the Probate Registry to help a personal representative obtain probate without recourse to a solicitor. Telephone the helpline on 0845 30 20 900. ,,

APPLY FOR PROBATE YOURSELF OR USE A SOLICITOR?

There are examples of people sorting out legal problems themselves and conducting quite complicated cases without legal help. Some 'litigants in person', as they are called, have taken cases to court alone, and many people have bought or sold a house without a solicitor. Whereas a litigant in person and a do-it-yourself house-buyer cannot expect special treatment from the other side, a personal representative will find that special arrangements are in place at the Probate Registry to help him or her obtain probate without a solicitor.

If you feel that you would like to undertake applying for a grant (either probate or letters of administration) yourself and then continue to administer the estate, first look at:

- **The chart on pages 90–1** for a step-by-step breakdown of what needs to be done.
- **The Probate Registry form PA2** for guidance on applying for probate without a solicitor. Download it from the Principal Probate Registry website on www.hmcourts-service.gov.uk. Click on the 'Forms and Guidance' tab and in the box 'Work type' go to 'Probate'.

In addition, ask yourself the questions overleaf. If you are going to continue along the DIY route, it would be as well to know the answers.

This all creates a dilemma for the DIY executor or administrator. Do you take on ull responsibility for the administration, including personal liability for any miscalculation of tax or misunderstanding of the law, or do you involve a solicitor who is not expected to make mistakes but who carries indemnity insurance in case he or she does?

In some cases you might find a solicitor who is willing to deal with your application for probate but who will agree to leave you to deal with the gathering in of assets and paying off liabilities once probate has been granted. In such cases, the solicitor should make it very clear where his responsibilities end and yours begin. In other cases, a successful DIY executor might engage a solicitor to deal with a post-death deed of variation (see pages 78–9) or a challenge from a dependant.

As with any DIY, you must make an honest appraisal of your knowledge and ability before taking on the administration.

When to use a solicitor

There are some good reasons as to why might be worth employing a solicitor, which are outlined here:

- **Any number of complexities** can arise in connection with the administration of an estate.
- **Often the personal representatives** are busy people, without the time to cope with the legal side of an administration and would not contemplate administering an estate without employing a solicitor.
- **The solicitor carries insurance** in case he or she makes a mistake. Another

executor making a mistake might be personally liable.

- **A good knowledge of the law** is essential when the deceased owned his or her own business, for instance, or was a partner in a firm, or was involved in an insurance syndicate, or where there is agricultural property, or when family trusts are involved.
- **The same applies** where, on an intestacy or under the will, some of the property is to pass to children who are under the age of 18. Their rights are called minority interests and particular legal problems can arise regarding them.
- **Another situation** that usually requires legal advice is one in which, on an intestacy, some long-forgotten relative is entitled to a share in the estate. The problems involved in tracing relatives who have apparently disappeared generally require careful handling, as does the situation if they are not found.
- **Homemade wills,** particularly on printed forms, sometimes contain ambiguities or irregularities that can create difficulties, and legal help about the interpretation may be needed to avoid errors. An executor who wrongly interprets a will and fails to distribute to a lawfully entitled beneficiary may well become financially liable for the consequences of his or her mistake.
- **A solicitor** should also be consulted if there is a possibility of anyone seeking a share, or a larger share, of the deceased's estate under the Inheritance (Provision for Family and Dependants) Act 1975.

Do you want to pursue the DIY route?

In addition to the chart on pages 90-1, the questions and statements below are aimed at helping you decide on whether you will pursue the DIY route, hire the services of a solicitor or do both.

❝Do you know what assets and liabilities relate to the estate (see pages 18-19)?❞

❝Can you establish if any income tax or Capital Gains Tax was due from the deceased at the date of their death (see page 136)?❞

❝Do you have details of all jointly owned property that forms part of the estate (even if it does not pass under the will or intestacy) (see page 134)?❞

Your liabilities

- Can you be sure that you have discovered all the liabilities? If not, you could be personally liable if any debts come to light after the estate has been distributed unless you have placed a statutory notice in the *London Gazette* (see page 135).
- If the will or the intestacy creates a trust, you (as executor or administrator) will be responsible for the administration of that trust.
- If you decide to carry out the administration of the estate without help from a solicitor or accountant and there are any trusts included in the estate, you will have to get to grips with the law of trusts, which is beyond the scope of this guide.

IHT decisions

- Was the deceased a beneficiary of any trust or settlement? If so, the capital value of that trust must be aggregated with the value of the estate to determine how much IHT must be paid.

- Does the value of the estate exceed the threshold for IHT? If so, you need to claim all the available allowances and reliefs to reduce the tax burden. IHT on land or houses can be paid by ten equal instalments over ten years.

- Is there any scope for saving IHT by making a post-death deed of variation of the testator's will?

If there are questions of IHT and a deed of variation, it is best to consult a solicitor. See also the *Which? Essential Guide* to *Giving and Inheriting* by Jonquil Lowe.

Potential problems

- Is anyone likely to challenge the validity of the will?

- Do you anticipate any claim being made under the Inheritance (Provision for Family and Dependants) Act 1975?

- In the case of an intestacy, can you construct a complete family tree? Are there any illegitimate or adopted children to be included?

- Has anyone died leaving children?

If your answer to any of these questions is 'I don't know' and nor do you know where to find the answers, it is probably best to seek the advice of a solicitor.

Negligence by executors and administrators

If the administration is being conducted by an executor who is also a solicitor, or if you have instructed a solicitor to deal with the administration for you, he or she is liable at law if he or she is negligent. A solicitor has to hold insurance to cover this possibility.

If you are a lay executor, always take advice when a problem crops up that you do not understand. You may otherwise be personally liable if things go wrong. If you act on advice from a solicitor (preferably in writing) and the advice is wrong, the solicitor is liable.

Solicitors' fees

A solicitor's fees for dealing with an estate are paid out of the deceased's property. They are a legitimate expense, like the funeral expenses and any IHT. The personal representatives do not have to pay them out of their own pockets: along with any other debts and taxes, legal costs are usually paid first from the assets of the estate, after which the remaining monies are distributed to the beneficiaries.

Solicitors should charge fees in accordance with the Solicitors' (Non-Contentious Business) Remuneration Order 1994. This sets out the elements that can affect the final fee, including the time spent, the complexity of the estate and its value. The order also sets out the rights of clients to information and interest.

Clearly, the charges will be considerably less for a straightforward administration

 If the estate is insolvent – if the debts exceed the value of the assets – great care is required; in fact, it's best to take advice from a solicitor. The same applies where, although the estate is solvent, there is not sufficient to pay all the legacies in full or there is no residue. If you arrange a funeral but there is no money in the estate to cover it, you will have to foot the bill.

“ Solicitor's fees are paid from the estate. ”

 There are various ways of raising money to fund a IHT bill. These are described on pages 127–8.

100

Get informed

The Law Society tells solicitors that they should give their clients the 'best information possible' about the likely costs when they take instructions, so do remember to ask at an early stage for a 'terms of business letter' if you are not told.

❝If a will states that a bank is to be the executor, talk to the bank early on to establish its fee scales – you might want to try to negotiate them down.❞

than for one in which complicated matters arise, although the solicitor may not know about them at the outset. Discuss with your solicitor how often you will be advised on progress (remember that you will be billed £12 or £20 for each letter or telephone call).

Bank fees

If the will states that a bank is to be the executor, it is worth talking to the bank at an early stage if you wish to challenge its fee scales, as banks tend to calculate their charges according to a percentage of the gross estate. Typical charges would be 5 per cent of the first £75,000 (£3,750), with 3 per cent levied on the next £50,000 (£1,500), and 2 per cent on any balance over £125,000. If the estate is under £10,000, a minimum charge of £500 may be levied, but there can also be additional fees.

TIMESCALES

An application for a grant of probate will not be accepted within seven days of a death and letters of administration within 14 days. If all the information is available and there is no IHT liability, your application might be dealt with in a couple of weeks. If the assets and liabilities are few and simple, you could perhaps have the job done within three or four weeks. However, life is seldom as simple as that. An administration can be delayed for a myriad of reasons:

- A post mortem is required.
- One of the executors is not immediately available.
- The will cannot be found or it is ambiguous.
- The testator's papers are in a mess.
- The solicitor is too busy to give priority to your matter.

For more information on IHT, see pages 111–12 (Calculating the share of a house for IHT), pages 127–8 (Raising money to pay IHT) and page 136 (IHT rectification).

101

- A dependant (child or ex-spouse or civil or other partner) is thinking of making a claim.
- Valuations have to be obtained but several of the share certificates cannot be found.
- The deceased is thought to have made recent gifts but no one knows the details.
- Time must be allowed for claimants to come forward.
- The deceased receives a payment from an old family trust every year but the trustees have not made a tax return for the past two or three years.
- One or more of the beneficiaries cannot be found and may have died.
- The family cannot decide what should happen to the family home.
- A tax return is required up to the death of the testator.
- Property has to be transferred.
- It looks as though someone may make a claim against the estate (they have six months from the grant to begin proceedings).

If you deal with the estate, you will have the advantage of knowing what is holding things up (let's hope you never have to do anything else or take a holiday until the job is done!).

❝With so many potential hitches, it is no wonder that the administration of some estates can take many months to complete. ❞

First actions

There is a Personal Application Department in each of the Probate Registries, which has special staff, forms and procedures designed to smooth the path of the inexperienced layman.

However, the help and advice given by the Personal Application Department is confined to getting the grant of probate or letters of administration, and thereafter the personal representative is generally left to carry out the rest of the administration without assistance (see pages 131–44).

In cases where IHT is payable, the Capital Taxes Office (a branch of HMRC) is geared up to help the layman, but you must take great care to ensure that a mistake or omission does not have financial consequences as these will fall on to your shoulders. You must have a clear understanding of what you are doing and what your obligations are; if you don't, consult a solicitor.

Executors and administrators owe a duty of the utmost faith not only to the deceased but also to the probate court, the creditors of the estate and the beneficiaries. They are under an obligation to realise the maximum benefit from the estate and can be challenged by the beneficiaries or the creditors if they fail to meet their obligations. Therefore, keep all matters of the administration of the estate entirely separate from your own personal affairs as you must be able to show, later on, by the preparation of estate accounts, that all the assets of the estate can be accounted for.

Before going any further, however, there are a few things that you should do early on in the proceedings.

> **❝ Executors and administrators owe a duty of the utmost faith not only to the deceased but also to the probate court, the creditors of the estate and the beneficiaries. ❞**

Having trouble finding your local probate registry? Go to website www.lawontheweb. co.uk/basics/probateoffices.htm, which lists each region in England and Wales. For the Capital Taxes Office, go to www.hmrc.gov.uk/inheritancetax.

OBTAIN COPIES OF THE DEATH CERTIFICATE

All deaths have to be registered, at which point the informant (the person registering the death) receives a death certificate. The most usual person to be the informant is:

- A relative of the deceased who was present at the death.
- A relative of the deceased who was present during the last illness.
- A relative of the deceased who was not present at the death or during the last illness but who lives in the district or sub-district where the death occurred.
- A person who is not a relative but who was present at the time of death.

An informant can also be an executor or administrator. If you are either of these but not the informant, ask the person who is the informant to ensure he or she obtains several copies of the death certificate when registering the deceased's death. Each copy costs £3.50 (2009) and three should be sufficient. For more information, see the *Which? Essential Guide* to *What to do When Someone Dies*.

ESTABLISH YOU HAVE FULL AUTHORITY

Establish from the will that you have full authority to act as an executor, which can be either singly or jointly. If you are a joint executor, decide who is going to do what and get this down in writing. Even if you divide responsibilities, you will still both have to sign the probate documents and claim forms. You are both legally responsible for the proper administration of the estate.

SEARCH THE CONTENTS OF THE DECEASED'S DEED BOX

If such a thing exists, documents might be stored in there, such as a life insurance policy, National Savings & Investments certificates, a building society account book, Premium Bonds and share certificates.

 Provided you keep the necessary receipts and a separate note of the amounts involved, executors and administrators are entitled to recover any expenses reasonably incurred in the administration of the estate. On the other hand, you cannot claim payment for time spent.

 Obtaining copies of a death certificate at a later date is a more complicated and expensive affair. Useful websites for doing so are: www.direct.gov.uk/gro (the General Register Office), www.groni.gov.uk (Registrar General, Northern Ireland) and www.gro-scotland.gov.uk (General Register Office, Scotland).

GET ORGANISED

t's worth setting up a large file with different sections for each organisation you will be contacting, e.g. bank, insurance company, building society. Take a copy of the will for the file, too. f the original gets damaged in any way, the Probate Registry might raise queries about it.

❝ Obtaining a few copies of the death certificate will stand you in good stead as you can then contact several companies or banks simultaneously. ❞

Safeguarding the deceased's property

In cases where the house has to remain empty after the death of its owner, it is important for the executor to safeguard the house and its assets. Do not go alone or you may be accused of taking items or money that other beneficiaries believe the deceased had in their possession.

- **Check the insurance** on the house is adequate and valid.
- **Remove any valuables** for safe keeping (don't forget to notify your own insurers if you are looking after the valuables). Make sure the other beneficiaries know what you are doing.
- **Advise the police** and see if a neighbour is willing to keep an eye on the house for you.
- **You may wish to keep the services running** but you might find that you

have to turn off the water to maintain insurance cover through the winter. Discuss the situation with the insurers to make sure you are as fully covered as possible.

- **If there is a car,** it will cease to be covered by the deceased's policy although, as a short-term measure, the insurers may agree to fire and theft cover if it remains in a garage.
- **Arrange with the post office** that all mail will be redirected to one of the executors. An application form can be obtained from any post office and a fee is payable depending on the number of months the service is needed. This forwarding service is particularly useful where a house will be standing empty.

Valuing the assets

Now that you know what is likely to be involved in administering the estate, write to all the banks, building societies and insurance companies to find out the value of each asset at the date of death. As you receive answers, draw up a list similar to the one shown opposite.

In these letters, request a claim form for signature by the executors and you should include:

- The relevant account or policy number.
- A description of the asset.
- The fact that you are the executor of the will of the deceased (name in full).
- The name of the co-executor, if there is one, and give his or her address.
- A death certificate (it needs to be an original, a photocopy will not suffice). Ask for it to be returned.
- The fact that you will be able to send an office copy of the grant of probate once you have received it.
- An enquiry as to whether it is a certificated holding (if you have no certificate).

❝Be very precise with notes regarding the estate's assets. ❞

BANK ACCOUNTS

In addition to obtaining the bank account details, establish if the deceased kept a deposit account at the branch and, if so, the balance at the date of death and the interest accrued to the date of death but not yet added to the account. The deceased might also have kept a deed box at the branch, or otherwise deposited any documents there, and this, too, is worth establishing now.

When a bank is given notice of a customer's death, cheques drawn on that account are returned unpaid with a note 'drawer deceased', and all standing orders or direct debit mandates cease.

- Any cheques drawn by the deceased but not met on presentation because notice of death has been lodged at the bank should be regarded as a debt due from the deceased to the payee.
- If any payments are to be made to the account, the amounts will be held by the bank in a suspense account for the time being.

Normally, a bank must not disclose to other people the details of how much is in a customer's account and what

Provisional details of a sample estate

Leave a column at the right-hand side blank so that you can fill in the actual figures alongside the estimates as they become known. Put this provisional list of assets at the front of a file for easy access.

Assets	£ estimated value	£ actual value
Cash, including money in banks, building societies and National Savings		
Household and personal goods		
Stocks and shares quoted on the Stock Exchange		
Stocks and shares not quoted on the Stock Exchange		
Insurance policies, including bonuses and mortgage protection policies		
Money owed to the person who has died		
Partnership and business interests		
Freehold/leasehold residence of the person who has died		
Other freehold/leasehold residential property		
Other land and buildings		
Any other assets not included above		
SUB-TOTAL		

Liabilities	£ estimated value	£ actual value
The funeral		
Household bills		
Building Society mortgage		
SUB-TOTAL		

	£ estimated value
Approximate net value of the estate (assets less liabilities)	

Estimated IHT

Net value of estate	
Less nil-rate band	**325,000**
Estimated IHT @ 40% =	

Cut all debit or credit cards in half so that they cannot be used fraudulently.

securities, deeds or other papers or articles are held, let alone hand them over. The exception is where the information is needed by the executors or administrators after a death so that the IHT accounts can be completed.

❝ A joint bank account need not be in equal shares. ❞

Joint bank accounts

When assets are held in joint names, it may be that the holders intended that, in the event of a death, that person's share would pass to the survivor.

If it is impossible to show who contributed what, or if the items in the account are too numerous or complicated to make it possible to distinguish the sources, the balance might be considered to be held equally by its joint holders.

However, where the joint account holders are husband and wife, it is presumed that even if all the money came only from the husband or only from the wife, it is held by them equally. Therefore, half the balance on the date of death would be taken as the value belonging to the spouse or civil partner who has died. Circumstances may also show that a joint account held by an unmarried couple is

owned equally between the joint account holders. It is best to settle any dispute in this area by agreement as the law can be vague on joint ownership, which is fertile ground for disputes.

A joint account held by a couple has the advantage that the survivor can continue to draw on the account even though the other account holder has died. As it can take weeks or even months to get a grant of probate, this allows the survivor to have continued access to ready cash.

The balance in a personal joint account will usually pass automatically to the survivor and so bypasses the will (unless it is a trust account or some other specific agreement was made between the joint account holders). Nevertheless, the share of the deceased is included as an asset of the estate for IHT purposes – unless the survivor is the surviving spouse or civil partner, in which case it is an IHT-exempt transfer.

With any assets held jointly, such as building society accounts, savings bank accounts and investments, similar principles apply. Joint accounts can produce difficult problems in assessing IHT.

Direct debits

Contact the companies concerned to explain there has been a death and so any direct debits will cease. Let them know that you will settle any outstanding payment when the probate has been granted (if the estate is solvent).

BUILDING SOCIETY ACCOUNT

When you write to a building society, enclose the passbook, if there is one, so that a note of the death can be made on it and to ensure there is no possibility of a fraudulent person making withdrawals on the account.

The amount shown in the book might not necessarily be the current balance of the account because of subsequent payments in or withdrawals, so it is best to ask for confirmation of:

- **The capital balance** at the date of death.
- **Interest due** but not added to the account at that date.
- **What interest was credited** to the account in the last tax year ending 5 April.

NATIONAL SAVINGS & INVESTMENTS (NS&I)

If there are any NS&I products, such as Savings Certificates and Premium Bonds, to realise:

- **Obtain claim form DNS 904** (Death of a holder of NS&I) from the post office.
- **Valuations of the various assets** will be returned to you together with repayment/transfer forms, depending on how you indicate the assets are to be dealt with.

Where the value of all NS&I Savings accounts or bonds (including interest and any Premium Bond prize won since the date of death – see box, below) is £5,000 or less, it may normally be paid out without any grant having been obtained. NS&I will, however, ask if

Premium Bonds

Premium Bonds do not need to have an official valuation, but you should nevertheless notify NS&I of the bondholder's death as soon as possible by filling in form NS&I904 (www.nsandi.com or telephone 0845 964 5000). Premium Bonds retain their face value, and no question of interest arises. They cannot be transferred to beneficiaries but may be left in the prize draws for 12 calendar months following the death, and then cashed. The money can be reinvested in new bonds in the name of the beneficiary, but these will have to wait three months before becoming eligible for inclusion in the prize draw.

Where it happens that a prize warrant has been paid into the deceased's bank account after the date of death but before either the bank or NS&I has been notified to freeze the account or stop payment, NS&I will ask for the prize to be returned so that a new warrant can be sent to the executors after probate has been registered.

a grant is being obtained and, if so, may refuse to pay without sight of it unless the savings were held jointly or in trust.

INSURANCE POLICY

Check through any insurance policy to establish what type it is. If it is a with-profits policy, an additional sum will be paid to you, the executor, by the insurance company. In this instance, when you write to the company with a death certificate, you should ask for confirmation of the amount payable on death in addition to the sum assured.

> **❝** How much you value a property will have implications if there is IHT to pay. In this instance, bring in a professional valuer. **❞**

Jargon buster

District valuer The district valuer is employed by HMRC but the job has little to do with taxes as such. He or she is concerned with the valuation of land, houses, factories, shops, offices and so on for many official purposes. He or she is an expert on valuation

VALUATION OF PROPERTY

Most people have some idea of the current value of the properties in their locality. It is not essential in the first instance to obtain a professional valuation from a firm of surveyors and valuers.

Whether you have a professional valuation or not, if the estate is large enough to incur IHT, your estimate will be checked sooner or later by an official called the **district valuer**. The district valuer knows the value of every sale in his or her district so there is no point in trying to understate the value of a house. However, for possible saving on IHT, at this stage you may decide to put down your lowest reasonable estimate of value. The district valuer may query your figure later on if it is too low, but perhaps not if it is on the high side. If there is IHT to pay on the estate, you would be wise to bring in a professional valuer to prepare a valuation in case the district valuer should challenge your valuation.

However (particularly in an estate where there is no IHT payable), pushing for a higher estimated value could mean less tax in the long run if there is a possibility that any future sale might be subject to Capital Gains Tax (CGT) (see pages 117–18). The established value for IHT purposes will be the beneficiary's base cost for CGT purposes, so a low IHT value on death might mean a larger gain on any future sale.

 If you live in Scotland, Scottish probate law is different in certain places to the law of England and Wales, so turn to pages 164-72 for changes in the law that you need to be aware of.

Where a house is not going to be sold, it is possible to agree its value with the district valuer before applying for probate, but this can delay matters.

If the property is jointly owned

There are two ways in which people may own a house or land jointly: as joint tenants or as tenants in common. Married couples and civil partners usually hold property as joint tenants, and business partners as tenants in common, but this isn't always the case.

- **Where a house is owned by joint tenants,** the share of the first to die (the shares are always equal) passes to the survivor automatically on death. The survivor of joint tenants acquires the other half-share merely by surviving, irrespective of anything the will may say.
- **In the case of tenants in common,** however, the share of the first to die passes according to the will or intestacy. It could pass to the co-owner

---

If there is any doubt as to whether the property is in the deceased's name alone or in joint ownership as a joint tenancy or tenancy in common, you must check what the deeds (or title) says, but this does not always produce the answer.

---

under the will, but that is not the same thing as the share passing to him or her automatically, as happens when it is a joint tenancy, and it may go to someone quite different. You will have to discover the proportions in which the tenancy is held (this could be unequal) in order to estimate the value of the share of the deceased at the date of death. This information may sometimes be found by referring to the deeds or the title if the land is registered because there may be a Declaration of Trust, which sets out the proportions of ownership for tenants in common. This document may not show up with the title deeds so proceed with care. In case of any doubt, seek professional advice.

Calculating the share of the house for IHT

Whenever a house is held in the joint names of two people (whether married or not) the value of the deceased person's share has to be declared for IHT purposes. The vacant possession value at the date of death is the starting point in calculating the value of the deceased's share of the house for IHT. Suppose it is the figure of £200,000. In the case of a joint tenancy or a tenancy in common held in equal shares, that figure must be divided by two to determine the share of the one who has died. This would give a figure of £100,000.

Except where the joint owners are husband and wife or civil partners, HMRC accept that the value of a part share in jointly held property is usually worth less than simply the relevant share of the vacant possession value. This is because on the open market it will generally be hard to find a buyer willing to buy just a part share, especially if the surviving co-owner(s) have the right to stay in the property.

As a starting point, HMRC allows you to reduce the value of the deceased's share of a property by 10 per cent. In the example above, therefore, the £100,000 share of the £200,000 house would be reduced to £90,000 for IHT purposes.

However, if the surviving owner has the right to stay in the property, HMRC should accept a 15 per cent reduction, which would mean that in this example,

the value of the deceased's share would be £85,000. Attempts have been made to establish even greater reduction but you would need a valuer in order to pursue that point.

Joint ownership by married or civil partners

Valuation officers do not allow any such reduction in the value because of what is called 'related property' provisions, which apply under the Inheritance Tax Act. However, if before the death the property was jointly owned by, say, brothers and sisters, or two or more friends, or parent and child, or any two people not married to each other, you should claim the reduction in the valuation.

Outstanding mortgage debts

Account must also be taken of any outstanding mortgage debt on jointly owned property. Suppose that it is £20,000; then the deceased's share of this debt would normally be half – that is, £10,000. The result would be that the value of the deceased's share of the house (see main text, above) less the mortgage debt would be £75,000, assuming 15 per cent discount.

If there is any outstanding mortgage on the property, you need to obtain an exact figure from the mortgage lender showing the position of the mortgage at the date of death.

If there is an endowment mortgage, you need to establish its position, too. When a house is given to a beneficiary, you must check if the gift is free of the mortgage or subject to it.

 For the Which? report on IHT, go to the Which? website: www.which.co.uk. Some of the content on the website is only available to subscribers – information for how to subscribe is given on the website. See also the *Which? Essential Guide* to *Giving and Inheriting.*

SHARES AND UNIT TRUSTS

For shares and unit trusts, you need to establish what their value was on the day of death.

You can find a rough estimate of what they were worth by looking up the closing prices in the paper. But for IHT purposes, it is necessary to know their exact price, for which you must refer to the Stock Exchange Daily Official List (SEDOL) (see box, below).

- **For an estate where no IHT is payable,** it is acceptable to use a newspaper for the right day (remember that the price of shares at the end of Monday 3 October is shown in the paper for Tuesday 4 October).
- **For an estate where IHT is payable,** shares and units trusts (and open-ended investment companys (OEICs)) must be valued correctly. You may work from a link on the Stock Exchange site at: www.londonstockexchange.com/information-providers/historical-data/valuation-data/validation-data.htm.
- **You can work it out for yourself** for a small number of shares from the SEDOL. The way to use the information is complicated and explained on the HMRC website

---

Death at a weekend

If the death was at the weekend, prices from the official list for the Friday or for the Monday may be used and you may mix the Friday and Monday prices to the estate's advantage.

---

at www.hmrc.gov.uk/cto/customerguide/page8-1.htm.

- **For unit trusts and OEICs** most managers will provide the information that you need free.

If there is a long list, it is probably better to write to the bank (but you will be charged for the valuation). Alternatively, a stockbroker would be able to provide this information quite easily, either on the telephone in the case of a few quotations, or by letter if there are more. When a stockbroker makes a valuation, his charge is based on a percentage of the value of the shares.

❝The value of shares and unit trusts has to be established for the day of death.❞

 Your local reference library may take SEDOL, as might a very large branch of a bank, or you can buy it for a relatively small sum from FT Information Services: www.ftid.com. There is a link from the Stock Exchange website to probate valuation information at www.londonstockexchange.com/information-providers/historical-data/valuation-data/validation-data.htm.

Checking the holdings

Check you have the correct holdings by writing to the registrar of each company concerned. The address of the registrar usually appears on the counterfoil of the dividend warrant. The counterfoil also acts as a certificate of Income Tax paid, so it is likely that these will have been kept in a safe place. If you can't find the counterfoils, it may be because the deceased didn't keep them, or they may be at the bank if the dividends were credited there directly from the company, or they may be with the deceased's accountant.

❝ If you can't find the share certificate(s), make a note to get hold of a duplicate from the relevant company once you have been granted probate. ❞

Watch out for uncertificated shares and unit trusts. If the deceased did not keep good records, you may easily miss some of his or her investments. Look carefully at all the paperwork.

If, after further searching, you still can't find the share certificate(s), make a note to get hold of a duplicate once you have been granted probate. To do this, you will have to contact the relevant company registrar (see box, below) and you will probably have to pay a fee. You also need to remember that some holdings may have a certificate while others may be uncertificated holdings, so check the records carefully.

Write the standard letter as outlined on page 106 and ask for confirmation of the relevant holdings and whether there is any unclaimed dividend or interest payment held at the offices.

When a company does not want to distribute its dividend but wishes to retain the cash within the company, it will sometimes 'capitalise' the dividend and instead issue additional shares (called a **bonus, or scrip, issue**).

A rights issue is when a company offers its shareholders further shares at less than the market price. If, at the date of death, payment for a rights issue is due, contact the registrar to see if he or she will agree to postpone payment until probate is received. If not, the funds would have to be raised elsewhere (from the bank or by a loan from the executors or beneficiaries to the estate), because the payment may secure a valuable asset to the estate. If payment is not made as required, the rights will be lost.

The same point could arise if a deceased person had just acquired shares in a newly privatised company. Sometimes the original subscription will be for only part of the price, and the

 To find a company registrar, the *Register of Registrars* gives details of the registrar of each company quoted on the stock exchange. It is held in some libraries, or telephone the head office of the companies concerned to find the proper address for the registrar.

Ex-dividend

If a price for shares has the letters 'xd' beside it, this means that the price was quoted 'ex-dividend'. This means that if the shares are sold, the seller – not the buyer – will receive the next dividend on these shares. The price the buyer pays is therefore lower than he or she would otherwise pay, to the extent of the dividend that is being foregone. This is because the company prepares the actual dividend cheques in advance in favour of the owner at that time, so if the shares are sold before the company sends out the cheque on the day the dividend is due, it will still go to the seller. This usually happens about six weeks before the date for payment of dividends.

Phone the registrar of the company (see box, opposite) to find out what the dividend to be paid is on each share. You can then calculate the total. The dividend must be included as an asset in the HMRC account of the estate if you receive it.

balance will be payable by the owner of the shares some months later. If the date is missed, the share can be forfeited or lost, so it is important to ensure that the money is available from some source. It is always wise to check the correct procedure with each company's registrar because practice can vary from company to company.

Unit trusts

If you own shares in one company, you do not know how well that company is going to perform and therefore what profits it will earn, which directly affects the value of the shares. Many people consider it sensible to spread the risk by owning shares in a number of larger companies.

Some investment managers have specialised in this, and it is possible to buy units in a pool of investments in which the investment managers specifically aim to spread the risk. With unit trusts, you do not buy and sell specific shares in companies but buy and sell a specific number of units. This 'unit trust' industry is itself very specialised; investment managers now deal in different funds so that units can be bought in a portfolio consisting, for example, of property companies, of UK companies or of overseas companies.

If the deceased owned such unit trusts, ask the trust manager to confirm the value of the holding on the date of death.

❝ When shares are spread across unit trusts, you will have to contact the trust manager to establish the value of the holding and the closing prices on the date of death. ❞

Private companies

Although older 'Ltd' certificates can still be valid, all companies whose shares are quoted on the stock exchange are now registered with the words 'Public Limited Company' or 'plc' at the end of the name. Private companies, whose shares are not quoted on the stock exchange (and which cannot always be freely sold), all have the word 'Limited' or 'Ltd' at the end of their name.

Valuing shares in a private company not quoted on the stock exchange requires expert help. Sometimes the secretary or accountant of the company concerned can state the price at which shares have recently changed hands, and this may be accepted for probate purposes. If not, detailed and possibly difficult negotiations may have to be undertaken and, unless the shares are of comparatively small value, it would be worthwhile to get an accountant to handle the matter. The basis of valuation is different depending upon whether the interest in the company is a minority or a majority shareholding.

❝ If any shares are in private companies whose shares are not traded on a regular basis, you would be wise to employ an accountant to establish their value. ❞

PENSIONS

Quite often a pension scheme provides that a capital sum should become payable on the death of one of its members. For instance, if a member were to die while still an employee – that is, before retirement – the scheme might provide for the return of the contributions that had been made over the years by the member, and from which he or she has derived no benefit, because he or she did not survive to collect the pension.

- **If the lump sum** that represents this return of contributions were part of the deceased's estate, it would have to be declared for IHT.
- **However, in most schemes** nowadays it would be paid 'at the trustees' discretion' and not be subject to IHT.
- **Such schemes provide that the trustees** may select who is to receive the capital sum (but they are bound by the rules of the particular scheme, and some are quite restrictive). However, schemes usually ask their members to fill in an 'expression of wish' form setting out the person or people they would like to receive the lump sum and the trustees will normally take this wish into account.
- **Provided the payment is made** genuinely at the trustees' discretion (and so the executors have no legal right to enforce the payment), there is normally no IHT regardless of to whom the payment is made. In very limited cases – for example, where the member was terminally ill and has

deliberately acted to increase the death benefit lump sum they leave – IHT could be due but not where the lump sum is left to a surviving spouse, civil partner or dependants.

Whatever the circumstances, it is wise, where the deceased belonged to a pension scheme, to get a letter from the secretary of the pension fund to confirm the exact position regarding what the estate (as distinct from a dependant) is entitled to receive under the scheme. Even if it is only the proportion of the pension due for the last few days of life, obtain a letter from the secretary so that you have written confirmation for the purpose of IHT.

State benefits

If the deceased was receiving state retirement pension and/or other state benefits, such as attendance allowance, winter fuel payment, pension credit or income support, report the death to the Pension Service or Jobcentre Plus using the form that will be given to you by the registrar when you register the death.

The Pension Service or Jobcentre Plus will work out if any arrears of payments are due. These form part of the estate. They have to be declared for IHT and included in the probate paperwork.

INCOME TAX AND CGT

Income Tax is usually based on a person's income received in the tax year that runs from 6 April to 5 April the following year. PAYE works so that a person's tax allowances are spread over the whole year and tax is deducted week by week, or month by month on the assumption that the taxpayer will go on having income throughout the year. If he or she dies during the year, the PAYE assumptions are upset because the taxpayer did not live to receive the income throughout the tax year, and a tax repayment will be due because the full year's allowances can then be set against the income to the date of death. Where the deceased paid tax through self-assessment rather than PAYE, too little or too much tax may have been paid through their payments on account up to the date of death. Also, if the taxpayer was not liable for tax because his or her income did not exhaust the allowances due, the estate may be

❝ The Pension Service and Jobcentre Plus will help you establish if any arrears of state benefit payments are due. ❞

For further information on benefits and allowances, go to the Department of Work and Pensions (www.dwp.gov.uk), HMRC (www.hmrc.gov.uk), Jobcentre Plus (www.jobcentreplus.gov.uk) or the Pension service (www.pensionservice.gov.uk).

entitled to a tax repayment where the deceased has received bank interest from which tax had been deducted. Any tax rebates must be included as part of the value of the estate.

You should explain the situation fully to the local inspector of taxes and, if necessary, go to see him or her about any repayment that may be due because too much Income Tax was levied on the deceased during the tax year in which he or she died. Although tax is claimed only on the amount of income that was received up to the date of death, tax allowances (such as a single person's or a married person's personal allowance) are granted for the full year, even if the death took place early in the tax year.

If the deceased had an accountant, it is sensible to ask him or her to complete the tax return to the date of death.

Depending on the circumstances, you are likely to receive a tax return or a tax claim for completion.

Income received after the date of death

Where income is received after the date of death, you, as the personal representative, will be taxed, either by prior tax deduction or by assessment in the normal way. You will not pay the higher tax rate but, on final distribution, you need to provide a certificate (R185) for the beneficiaries showing what tax has been deducted from the income that is being passed on to them – see page 136.

Strictly speaking, you should notify HMRC within six months of the relevant year-end and complete a tax return. However, HMRC has recently extended its informal procedure to cover straightforward estates whose income for the administration period does not exceed £10,000. In these cases, the personal representatives can submit a simple computation of the tax liability. In other cases, a self-assessment return will be required.

66 The local inspector of taxes will let you know if any repayment may be due for the tax year in which the testator died. **99**

 You are given no personal allowances to set against the estate income, but you can off set against the income any interest paid on a loan raised to pay the IHT.

 As with all forms from HMRC, it is possible to download form R185 from the HMRC website: www.hmrc.gov.uk/pdfs/r185.pdf.

CONTENTS OF PROPERTY AND PERSONAL ASSETS

The next item requiring valuation is the furniture and effects. This includes:

- Furniture in the property
- Household goods of all kinds
- Jewellery
- Clothes
- The car
- All personal possessions.

It may not be necessary to prepare a complete list, or to state the respective values of different kinds of articles – but the Capital Taxes Office (who deal with IHT) are becoming more interested in the value of personal belongings and household contents.

Where the person who has died was sharing the house with a spouse or civil partner, it is important to realise that it is only the deceased's own household goods, effects, furniture and so on, which need to be included in the list of items passing under the will. A husband and wife may have regarded all of the property as being jointly owned by the two of them so that, on the death of either, it becomes wholly owned by the survivor. In such a case, one-half of the value of all the contents should be shown as passing to the survivor. If the deceased owned any particular items outright, the full value of those items will have to be included. (There may be specific items bought by the husband or the wife particularly for him or herself, or acquired by way of inheritance from their own respective families. Such items could quite possibly have been regarded by them as belonging to one or the other, not jointly held.)

You should discuss the matter with the other person concerned to ascertain precisely what was owned by the deceased, what was owned by the other person and what was jointly held.

It will usually be assumed that, in the case of a husband and wife, the items are jointly held. If property is held by joint tenants who are not married or in a civil partnership, it will become owned by the surviving owner regardless of the provisions of the will or intestacy, although part of the value will have to be declared for tax purposes. In the case of unmarried couples, it is usually assumed that the person who paid for an item owns it. Obviously, the provisions in a will (or indeed, intestacy) can operate only on the property that is found to be part of the deceased's estate, and no tax is payable on anything owned by someone else.

Valuing a car

The make and age of the car are the principal factors that affect its value; its condition is another consideration. A study of the prices being asked for second-hand cars by local garages or dealers will give an indication of the value to within about £50. There are also magazines, such as *What Car?*, that detail values of new and used cars. Do not forget to deduct any outstanding loan. If the car is on hire purchase, contact the hire purchase company to obtain its consent to sale (see also box on page 121).

Valuing jewellery

For probate purposes, it is the value for which jewellery could be sold that is needed; insurance value would be the cost of replacement, which is often considerably higher. You will have to pay a valuation fee, for which the jeweller will give you a receipt at the same time as the official valuation certificate. The fee can be included in expenses recovered from the estate due to you as personal representative.

Photographic evidence

HMRC pays particular attention to the estimated open-market values given for household and personal goods, so be ready to support your estimates with written and photographic evidence. It even looks at car registration numbers for additional value.

Valuing paintings

When making a calculation of the total value of the effects, it is better to put a separate valuation on items of particular value, such as, say, paintings worth more than £100. This can be reasonably easy to establish, perhaps because they were recently purchased or had been valued by an expert for insurance (although the insurance value is unlikely to be the same as the probate value). If not, you can obtain a verbal estimate of their sale value by taking them to a local auction house.

General valuation

More difficult to fix is a value for the great bulk of the household furniture and effects. How do you decide what the tables, chairs, beds, linen, cups and saucers, carpets, TV set, clothes and all the rest of it are actually worth?

You have to decide what price they would get if sold to best advantage on the day of death. In practice, this means what they would fetch at an auction. Of course, the second-hand

❝ It is best to itemise any valuable jewellery and/or paintings. Other items can be included as a general valuation. ❞

Don't forget the cash

Cash is an asset – don't forget to gather any together and add it to your calculations.

On page 107 there is a chart to show the provisional details of a sample estate. Continue to refer to it and fill in for your own needs as it gives you prompts for such things as deducting funeral expenses and household bills.

Hire purchase

If there are any items being bought on hire purchase, it is sufficient to take a common-sense attitude by valuing the article as if it had been part of what the deceased owned, along with everything else, and then to treat any outstanding instalments as a debt due from the estate. Where the figures are large - for example, on a car - it might be better to declare the net value as an asset after deducting the outstanding debt, rather than bringing this in as a separate debt.

DEBTS AND LIABILITIES

If anyone owes money to the deceased, include it in the list of property declared for IHT, as these count as assets. They are debts due to the estate. Items such as the dividend on any shares, pensions due to the date of death and any income tax repayment fall within this category.

Debts due from the deceased have to be listed, too. Any money that is owed reduces the estate for the purpose of calculating the total value: the liabilities are deducted from the assets. These debts can consist of almost anything: fuel bills, tax, telephone account, amounts due on credit cards or credit accounts, hire-purchase debts, an overdraft, for example.

value of the great majority of items is considerably less than the cost when they are new.

For IHT, you do not consider the cost of replacement, but the price they would fetch if sold second-hand. The Capital Taxes Office of HMRC does not expect you to provide an expert's valuation on a non-IHT paying estate, or one that is accurate to within a few pounds, but a valuation that is honest and sensible, and says what the executor really thinks the items are worth. If the estate is liable to IHT, expect HM Revenue & Customs to question the accuracy of estimated values.

In some cases, debts can be a big problem in administering an estate. If you discover that the estate is insolvent, do not continue with the administration and take advice immediately from an insolvency adviser or from a Citizens Advice Bureau (see box, below), an accountant or a solicitor. It may be necessary to petition the court immediately for a trustee to be appointed to administer the estate - otherwise, you may become liable for the administrative costs and the funeral expenses if you have authorised them.

To find your nearest Citizens Advice Bureau (CAB), see your local phone book or go to www.adviceguide.org.uk.

In addition, the funeral expenses are deducted for IHT purposes (but not your expenses for administering the estate).

You will need to contact any companies and individuals that are owed money to check the amount owed and explaining that they will be paid soon after probate is granted (if you are sure the funds will be adequate).

MOVING TOWARDS APPLYING FOR PROBATE

As you receive answers from your letters to the bank, building society, etc., so you can start filling in the right-hand column of the deceased's list of assets and liabilities on page 107. Once you've heard from everyone – this could take about a month – you can complete the forms that enable you to apply for the grant of probate.

First, though, open an executor's account at your bank, so that you have somewhere specific to transfer money relating to the estate which is separate from your own bank account.

❝The next stage of obtaining probate requires a lot of form filling - you will be glad of your well-organised file and facts and figures. ❞

Probate application forms

Do not be deterred by the many forms and booklets listed below relating to applying for probate. They are all clearly laid out and designed to make the job as straightforward as possible. The information given in this chapter also applies to someone seeking letters of administration.

There are several forms to obtain when applying for probate. From the Probate Registry (see box at foot of page 124) you need the following documents:

- PA1: The probate application form
- PA1a: Guidance notes
- PA2: A guide to help a person applying for probate without a solicitor
- PA3: A list of probate fees
- PA4: A list of probate registries and interview venues.

If the value of the estate is no more than £325,000 (2009–10) (or no more than £1 million and left largely to a spouse, civil partner and/or charity), from the Capital Taxes Office at HMRC (see also box at foot of page 124) you need:

- IHT205: Return of estate information
- IHT206: Notes to help fill in IHT205.

If the value of the estate is more than £325,000 (2009–10) (including the deceased's share of any jointly owned assets, the value of assets held in trust and any gifts made within the last seven years – see pages 31–2), from the Capital Taxes Office at HMRC you will need:

- IHT400: The Inland Revenue account
- IHT421: Probate summary
- IHT400 Notes: to help fill in IHT400
- Supplementary pages
- IHT400 Calculation: A worksheet to work out the tax
- IHT423 (see page 127)
- C4: Corrective account (see pages 133 and 136)
- IHT30: Clearance certificate (see page 136).

There is a list of valuable information on the website of HMRC: www.hmrc.gov.uk/inheritancetax/iht-probate-forms/index.htm.

- Filling in the probate application form (PA1): Use the guidance notes from PA1a. This is an interactive form and can be filled in on-screen.
- Filling in the return of estate information (IHT205): Use the guidance notes from IHT206. If you can't determine the exact value of all items, reasonable estimates are acceptable (mark as 'estimated').
- Filling in the Inland Revenue account (IHT400): Use the guidance from IHT400 Notes. You can either assess any tax due yourself or ask HMRC (Capital Taxes) to do it for you (see box, below opposite).

> **❝ It is only the Probate Registries that will accept the completed forms. The Interview Venues exist precisely for the interviews, which occur later in the proceedings (see page 129). ❞**

RETURNING THE FORMS

If no IHT is payable, you must send the completed forms PA1 and IHT205 to the Probate Registry that controls the venue at which you wish to be interviewed (see form PA4 for addresses and venues). If IHT is payable, do not send IHT400 to this address; it has to be returned to HMRC (Capital Taxes) (see box, opposite top). With the forms you also need to send:

- A cheque or postal order made out to 'HMCS' (Her Majesty's Court Service) for the application (£90 in 2009) together with any other fees that are applicable (see form PA3)
- The original will and codicil(s) (if there are, keep copies)
- An official copy of the death certificate
- Any other documents requested on PA1

! The Probate and Inheritance Tax Helpline on 0845 30 20 900 is there to help you with ANY questions you may have, whether they are on obtaining forms in the first place; how to fill them in; how to find your nearest Controlling Probate Registry and Interview Venues. Use them!

 The forms from the Probate Registry can be obtained from www.hmcourts-service. gov.uk/cms/wills.htm or telephone the helpline 0845 30 20 900. The HMRC forms can be downloaded from their website: www.hmrc.gov.uk/inheritancetax.

IHT400: where and when to send it

If you want HMRC (Capital Taxes) to work out the tax for you:

- Send form PA1 together with any other documents needed and form IHT421 to the Controlling Probate Registry.
- Form IHT421 will be returned to you together with your appointment letter.
- Send form IHT400, supplementary pages and form IHT421 to HMRC (Capital Taxes Office), who will tell you what to do next.

If you have worked out there is IHT to pay:

- Fill in Sections B and C of form IHT421, copying the details from form IHT400.
- Then follow the procedure as above.
- When you send forms IHT400 and IHT421 to the Capital Taxes Office, enclose your IHT payment at the same time.
- The Capital Taxes Office will endorse form IHT421 and return it direct to the Probate Registry, who will issue the grant when your application is completed.

If you have worked out there is no IHT to pay:

- Follow the procedure as though there is IHT to pay – but minus the payment!

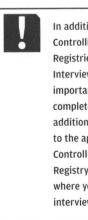

In addition to the Controlling Probate Registries, there are Interview Venues. It is important that you send the completed forms and additional documents only to the appropriate Controlling Probate Registry, depending on where you would like to be interviewed.

On the back of PA1 you will also be asked how many official copies of the grant you would like. This will vary depending on the size of the estate and how quickly you would like to finish the administration. The more copies you have, the more people you will be able to write to simultaneously. For an average estate, five copies (each costing £1) should be sufficient. If the estate incurs IHT, then something like ten copies might be appropriate.

The flowchart overleaf shows the sequence of events.

Some forms and guidance booklets differ in Scotland and it is important to obtain the correct set of forms or guidance booklets for the estate you are dealing with (see page 167). Full details are obtainable from www.hmrc.gov.uk.

Steps involved in the granting of probate

Send forms PA1, IHT421, the death certificate, the original will (keep a copy) and a cheque to cover the fee to the Probate Registry

↓

Attend an interview and collect completed form IHT421 from the Probate Registry, unless it was returned ahead of the interview and swear the executor's oath

↓

If there is IHT to pay, send form IHT400 and supplementary pages to the Capital Taxes Office together with form IHT421

↓

If there is any tax to pay, the Capital Taxes Office will advise you of the sum due

↓

Make payment of IHT to the Capital Taxes Office, following which it will send a receipted form IHT421 to the Probate Registry

↓

The Probate Registry will send you the grant of probate

If there is no IHT to pay

RAISING MONEY TO PAY IHT

Generally, assets cannot be dealt with before there is a grant of probate (or letters of administration). But if the person who died had a bank or building society account, it is possible that the bank or society will release money from the account for the purpose of providing finance for IHT (and funeral and probate fees). A cheque will be issued not to you, as executor or administrator, but made payable to HMRC for the IHT

and to the Paymaster General for the probate fees.

The Capital Taxes Office provides form IHT423 on which to apply to a bank for the IHT to be paid out of the deceased's account. The notes that accompany the forms explain how to fill them in and what to do with them.

If the person who died had a Girobank account, you may, subject to identification, borrow for the purpose of paying IHT, so that a grant of probate may be obtained. The borrowing is limited to solvent estates and to the amount of the credit balance in the deceased's account.

If this arrangement is not available, you will have to persuade a bank to give you a loan to cover the tax, which can then be repaid once probate has been granted. This can prove difficult if you do not have a friendly bank.

> ❝ IHT owed on a property can be paid by equal annual instalments over ten years. ❞

Paying the IHT on property by instalment

If there is property to sell that makes up a significant part of the value of the estate, this can reduce the tax payable before getting probate because land and houses are eligible for an instalment option. This means that the IHT due on the value of a house can be paid by ten equal instalments over a period of ten years. Interest is payable, but the first payment does not have to be made for six months. As a result, you may not have to raise a loan from the bank, although you will have to pay IHT on the value of the rest of the estate before you get the grant of probate that gives you access to the assets of the estate. If the house is sold within the ten years, all outstanding IHT must be paid.

You should have been sent form IHT421 with IHT400 (see page 123), but if not, go back to the Capital Taxes Office at www.hmrc.gov.uk/inheritancetax.

In theory, you can be faced with an odd dilemma. On the one hand, no bank or insurance company that holds money belonging to the estate is willing to hand any of it over to you until a grant of probate is obtained and produced to them; the probate is the only authority that can allow them to part with the money. On the other hand, you cannot obtain a grant of probate until you have actually paid the IHT, or at least most of it. How can you pay the tax without being able to get your hands on the wherewithal to pay it?

- **If there are funds** in NS&I accounts (and funds cannot be made available from anywhere else), these can be used to pay the IHT.
- **Also you can use:**
  - NS&I certificates
  - Yearly-plan and Premium Bonds
  - British savings bonds
  - Government stocks on the UK Debt Management Office (DMO) register, administered by Computershare
  - Money from save-as-you-earn contracts.
- **A special system** operates between the Personal Application Department of the Probate Registry and NS&I, which

enables this to be done – enquire at your local Probate Registry.
- **For obtaining payment** from a building society, see page 109.

For contact details, see the box, below.

"There are various means at your disposal for raising the cash to pay an IHT bill. "

For information on NS&I accounts, certificates and Premium Bonds, go to www.nsandi.com. For Computershare, go to www-uk.computershare.com.

AT THE PROBATE REGISTRY

Following the submission of the application for probate, you are given an appointment for an interview at the Controlling Probate Registry or Interview Venue that you requested at the top of form PA1. The purpose of the appointment is to confirm the information sent in the application and it should last no longer than 15 minutes. You can bring a friend or relative with you, if you like.

You will have to bring two separate forms of identification with you from the following list:

- Full driving licence
- Passport
- Bus pass
- National insurance card or National Health card
- State pension notification letter
- Child benefit notification letter
- A letter or invoice from a utilities company showing your current address
- Community tax bill.

> **!** Although the death certificate will be returned to you, the original will can't be returned. Instead, you will receive an official copy of the will with the grant. The original is kept by the Probate Registry and becomes part of public records.

" When you attend the interview at the Probate Registry, you must take two separate pieces of identification with you. "

All the information that you have supplied will have been translated on to a formal printed legal document, known as the executor's oath. The commissioner will ask you to check the forms to ensure the details are correct – as personal representatives, the executors are responsible for checking that everything is accurately stated (it's worth taking your file of papers with you).

Once you are satisfied that everything is in order, sign the oath in the space provided at the end. You will also need to sign the original will and finally swear on oath (or affirm) that the contents of the documents are true. It is a serious offence if you swear or affirm that the contents of the documents are true when you know they are not.

- **If IHT is payable,** you will be given form IHT421 to send with your IHT400 form to the Capital Taxes Office. If all is in order, they will advise you what tax to pay. Once you have paid the tax, the receipted IHT421 will be sent to the Registry, who will then issue probate.
- **If no IHT is payable,** the grant will then be posted to you, usually within ten working days of the appointment, together with copies you have paid for.

THE GRANT: PROBATE OR LETTERS OF ADMINISTRATION

While there may be an interval of several weeks between lodging the probate papers and being asked to come to the Probate Registry to sign and swear them, after that things tend to move quickly.

- **If there is no IHT to be paid,** the grant of probate (or letters of administration) will be issued within a few days.
- **If arrangements have to be made to pay the IHT,** matters might take a little longer.

Any property that passes by survivorship does not 'devolve to' the personal representatives but goes automatically to the survivor. (This is why it is excluded from the value of the personal estate even though it is not excluded from calculations for IHT, where applicable.)

At the end of the grant, the value of the gross and net estate (that is, before and after deduction of debts) is stated, but the amount of tax is not disclosed. The press often publish in the newspapers the value of the estates of famous people who have died. It is seldom a true indication of their wealth because it takes no account of any jointly owned property nor of any trusts to which they were entitled, nor, for that matter, of the IHT to be paid out, which will reduce the estate.

Attached to the grant of probate will be a photocopy of the will, accompanied by a note that briefly explains the procedure for collecting in the estate and advises representatives to obtain legal advice in the event of any dispute or difficulty.

You are now entitled to deal with the deceased's property, pay his or her debts and then distribute the property in accordance with the will – see pages 131–44.

Remember that the will is a public document in the sense that anybody, including any beneficiary, and even the press, can obtain a copy of it from the Principal Registry of the Family Division (see box, below) for a small fee. Copies of the will or the grant can also be obtained at the Probate Registry where they were issued.

> **❝A will is a piece of public property, so anyone can see it – for a fee – once probate has been granted. ❞**

All wills since 1858 are indexed at the Principal Registry of the Family Division. For more information about accessing copies of wills, to to www.courtservice.gov.uk/cms/1226.htm.

The administration

Applying for and receiving probate can take several months of preparation and correspondence, but by this stage the end is in sight. As soon as probate is granted, the assets can be realised, all creditors can be paid, tax affairs finalised and beneficiaries given their dues.

Example of how the final accounts might look

These accounts use the 2009-10 nil-rate band of £325,000 and assumes that none of the nil-rate band was previously used up by lifetime gifts. They also assume deceased is a single person - there is no double allowance from the spouse or civil partner's unused nil-rate band.

CAPITAL ACCOUNT

Assets (£s)

Property	227,500.00
Retained shares	85,550.00
Jewellery (valued)	1,500.00
Car (estimated)	4,000.00
Contents of the property (estimated)	11,000.00
Cash - endowment policy	85,300.00
life policy	9,100.00
building society	81,000.00
bank	1,900.00
NS&I certificates	5,000.00
Premium Bonds	4,000.00
1,500 units Investment Fund (sold)	2,730.00
£50,000 5% Treasury Stock 2008 (sold)	51,000.00
private pension arrears	200.00
state benefit arrears	78.00
cash	80.00
ASSETS TOTAL	**569,938.00**

Liabilities (£s)

Funeral account*		2,200.00
Household bills*		320.00
Mortgage on a property		25,400.00
Probate fees		140.00
Executor's expenses		200.00
Land Registry fees		70.00
Guarantee for missing share certificates		35.00
Inheritance Tax 1st payment	54,408.70	
2nd payment (payment on a property)	32,358.50	
Total Inheritance Tax		86,767.20
LIABILITIES TOTAL		**115,132.20**
Balance transferred to distribution account (assets less liabilities)		**454,805.80**

INCOME ACCOUNT

Received (£s)	Tax	Net
Building society	25.00	100.00
Dividend from shares	44.00	396.00
Interest – executor's bank account	7.50	30.00
TOTALS	76.50	526.00
Transfer to distribution account		526.00

THE DISTRIBUTION ACCOUNT

Received (£s)

Balance of £454,805.80 from Capital Account made up as follows:

Any property	227,500.00	
Retained shares	85,550.00	
Jewellery	1,500.00	
Car	4,000.00	
Contents	11,000.00	
Cash balance (cash less liabilities)	125,255.80	
(as a check, this should equal assets less liabilities)		454,805.80
Balance from income account		526.00
		455,331.80

Distribution (£s)

Legacies e.g. grandchildren (£500 each)		1,500.00
– a charity*		100.00
1st beneficiary: a car	4,000.00	
the contents of a property	11,000.00	
a property	227,500.00	242,500.00
The residue: 2nd beneficiary: ¹/₂ shares (value)	42,775.00	
¹/₂ balance	62,840.90	105,615.90
3rd beneficiary: ¹/₂ shares (value)	42,775.00	
¹/₂ balance (less jewellery, valued at £1,500)	61,340.90	
jewellery, valued at £1,500	1,500.00	105,615.90
		455,133.42

In the capital account, include the capital balance in the building society account at the date of death and interest accrued to that date. The income account includes any interest accrued after the date of death. The other interest payment represents the further interest due to the date of closing of the executor's deposit account.

In the income account, include the receipts of all the income received after the date of death, so they are excluded from the account to avoid recording the same item twice.

After legacies, the will gave the house free of tax and morgage and its contents to one beneficiary together with the car, and the balance was divided between two other beneficiaries, to one of whom the jewellery was appropriated.

* Figures are deductible before IHT is calculated.

IF THERE ARE CHILDREN BUT NO SURVIVING SPOUSE OR CIVIL PARTNER

In this instance, the children share everything (statutory trusts apply, see box, below).

The statutory trusts

Statutory trusts are:

- Any property due to the children of a person who has died intestate is to be held on trust for them provided they are living at the date of death of the intestate and that they attain 18 (or marry under that age).
- If a child of the intestate has died before the intestate but has left issue, then such issue will inherit the share of the deceased parent. The share will be divided if there is more than one of them.

IF THERE IS NO SPOUSE OR CIVIL PARTNER AND NO CHILDREN OR OTHER ISSUE

The estate is then taken by the relatives of the deceased in the following order:

1 Parents of the deceased
2 Brothers and sisters of the whole blood or their issue
3 Brothers and sisters of the half-blood or their issue
4 Grandparents
5 Uncles and aunts of the whole blood or their issue
6 Uncles and aunts of the half-blood or their issue
7 The Crown.

❝Statutory trusts were developed to protect the interests of any children involved in the estate.❞

Problems and disputes

Problems arise in many guises when administering a will, most of which can be relatively easily solved. Others are more difficult and require legal advice. This section aims to clarify those issues that arise the most frequently.

The most common problems

It is a sad fact that the death of a family member can trigger a dispute within the family. Another sad fact is that the cost of a dispute can reach astronomical levels and consume the value of the estate that is in dispute.

However, disputes do arise and have to be dealt with. The first sign of trouble is often preceded by the remark 'It's not the money that I'm bothered about. It's the principle of the matter.'

Disputes fall into two main categories. First, there are disputes over the will. Was it valid? Was it fair? Was it forged? Has it been destroyed by someone? Second, disputes can arise over the administration of the estate of the deceased person. Are the executors or administrators acting improperly or failing to do what they should be doing? Have they paid out to the wrong person or are they refusing to tell the beneficiaries what they have done? This section deals with both kinds of problems, and also includes a section on common misconceptions (pages 150–1).

If you are involved in a dispute over a will or administration, the best advice you will get is to try to settle it as quickly as possible, and perhaps to have a word with the Probate Registry (see box, below). If that cannot be done, you will almost certainly need to instruct a solicitor who knows his or her way around court procedures.

❝ Disputes over the will generally fall into these categories: is it valid, is it fair or is it forged? Or they involve an executor or administrator acting negligently or improperly. ❞

 To contact the Probate Registry, go to www.hmcourts-service.gov.uk. Their helpline phone number is 0845 30 20 900, and there are plenty of articles on the website that might address your particular problem.

PROBLEMS WITH THE WILL

Executors responsible for an estate and getting probate for it before distribution to the beneficiaries are strictly regulated by law. They also face problems that can impede progress and can also mean, at the worst, that the rules of intestacy apply.

No will can be found

The deceased person may never have made a will, but what if a member of the family believes that he or she did make one and it cannot be found? If a thorough search of papers and possessions fails to discover the will, one step is to write to local firms of solicitors and banks who might have been employed to make or keep a will on the deceased's behalf. If all enquiries fail, the rules of intestacy apply.

> ❝ The rules of intestacy come into force when no will can be found despite thorough searches. ❞

Jargon buster

Affidavit A declaration in writing made upon oath before someone who is authorised to administer oaths

The will doesn't appear to have been signed properly

Check the will carefully to ensure it has been signed by the testator and that the testator's signature has been witnessed by two witnesses (who must not be beneficiaries to the will). Both witnesses must have been present when the will was signed.

Q *I'm the executor for my mother's estate, but I'm not sure that it really is her signature on her will. What should I do about it?*

A As executor, if you have any doubts about the signing of the will, check with the witnesses. If the will has not been properly signed and witnessed, the Probate Registrar may declare it invalid or at the very least require a sworn **affidavit** to explain the irregularity.

The will isn't dated

If it is not dated, you have a problem. Do the witnesses remember when it was signed? If so, the Probate Registry will require an affidavit to explain the lack of a date. Sometimes it is apparent that a will has been changed or that some other document has been attached. Take all the documentation you have to the Probate Registrar, who can advise whether any of it should be counted as part of the will.

See pages 59–60 for the correct procedures for signing, dating and witnessing a will.

Is it the last will?

Even if you find a will that is properly dated and witnessed, it may not necessarily be the last will the deceased made. The older the will, the greater the chance that a later will or a codicil exists changing its terms. Always make further enquiries to be sure. Remember, too, that even an apparently valid will may have been wholly or partly invalidated by a subsequent marriage or divorce.

Q *My father remarried but I don't think he changed his will. Does the existing one remain valid?*

A Remarriage automatically revokes any earlier will unless that will was specifically stated to be made in contemplation of the marriage (see page 81). In particular, if there are children and a new will wasn't made following a remarriage, the rules of intestacy will automatically operate after death (see pages 143–4), so if your father's second wife is still alive, she will inherit the first £250,000 of the estate.

> ❝ Remarriage automatically revokes any earlier will unless that will was specifically stated to be made in contemplation of the marriage. ❞

TESTATOR PROBLEMS

As well as problems with the form of the will, there might also be queries relating specifically to the testator.

The testator doesn't appear to have had 'testamentary capacity'

In order to make a valid will, a testator must understand what he or she owns, understand the effect of the will and recognise individuals to whom he or she might have responsibilities – for instance, a wife with young children. As claimant, if you believe the testator lacked testamentary capacity, you need medical evidence to support your case and should take legal advice.

The testator may have been threatened or improperly influenced

Anyone wishing to challenge the will on these grounds must show that the testator was induced to make it by force, fear or fraud or that in some other way the will was not made voluntarily. Take legal advice before attempting to challenge a will on these grounds.

If someone decides to challenge the will, he or she may apply to the Probate Registry for a 'caveat'. This prevents an application for probate being made. It covers all registries and lasts for six months. If not renewed, it lapses. While it is in force, probate cannot be issued. If a caveat has been registered, as executor, you first have to resolve the problem with the applicant. If you cannot, you have to issue a warning to the Probate Registry, which has the effect of beginning a court action to settle the dispute. This is an area requiring specialist knowledge, so seek legal advice at an early stage.

Q *My sister lived near to my mother and got her to make a will leaving my sister a much larger share of the estate than she left to me. Can I challenge the will?*
A It depends; If your mother had testamentary capacity and was not coerced into giving your sister a larger share, she has every right to decide for herself who gets what. Perhaps she felt a moral obligation to compensate your sister for looking after her. If, on the other hand, you can obtain medical evidence to prove that your mother did not have testamentary capacity or if you can obtain evidence to show that your mother made her will as a result of threats by your sister, then you may well be able to challenge the will. You should take legal advice in such cases. It is possible also to challenge a will on grounds of undue influence.

The will or distribution on intestacy is unfair

If it is generally agreed by the beneficiaries that the will (or intestacy) has not made reasonable provision for all the interested parties, they can enter into a deed of variation (see pages 78–9). This has the effect of rewriting the will or intestacy rules. This step must be taken within two years of the death. If the variation reduces the share of a beneficiary who is under 18, the court's approval must be obtained.

If you wish to make such an agreement, take legal advice. If there is no agreement and the matter remains in dispute, the only recourse is to take the dispute to court. Probate actions can be very expensive, in effect transferring a substantial proportion of the estate from the beneficiaries to their solicitors and barristers. If there is no alternative, the claimant has to take proceedings under the Inheritance (Provision for Family and Dependants) Act 1975.

❝ A court action to settle a dispute calls for legal advice. ❞

Q *My Dad made his own will leaving the house to me and the money to my sister. The house looks out onto a large farmyard around which there are several barns that could get planning permission for conversion to dwellings. The house and all the farm buildings are on the same deed but my sister says I should only get the house. My sister also says that my Dad's pension fund and investment portfolio should be included with the money he had in the bank, but I'm not so sure that is what my Dad intended. There is also the issue of Inheritance Tax. Can I challenge the will?*
A The will is certainly ambiguous so you will have to establish what your father intended his will to say. Your first step should be to try to agree a meaning with your sister. If that fails, you will have to take the matter before a court for a decision and accept that several thousand pounds will disappear in legal costs.

Common misconceptions

My unmarried brother didn't make a will, but before he died he wrote me a letter to say he didn't want our sister to get anything from his estate. As I am my brother's administrator, can I leave my sister out?

No. The letter does not override the testamentary provisions.

My mother's will left everything to be divided between me and my brother, but as my brother died some years ago, does everything come to me?

If your brother had no children, you would inherit everything. But if he had children, they will share what their father would have inherited had he survived your mother, unless the will says otherwise.

Are all debts cancelled when a person dies?

No, none are cancelled although some credit card debts and mortgages may be covered by life insurance, in which case the insurance money can repay the debt. (Watch out for some wills that leave a house to one person and any insurance policies to another. This can mean that the person who gets the house also gets the mortgage debt.)

My brother borrowed £10,000 from my mother before she died but he says it was a gift and won't pay it back to her estate.

This is a problem. In order to challenge your brother's assertion you will need evidence to show that it was a loan. Without written evidence you will struggle to convince a court that it was a loan.

did my mother's probate myself and had
~~end a lot of time on it. Can I make a
~~ge for the time I have spent as I had to
time off work? **"**

. A lay executor is not entitled to any remuneration, although you
~ entitled to be reimbursed for any reasonable expenses you incur,
~h as petrol and telephone.

" As executor of my mother's will I have to look
after a large sum for my nephews until they are
21. As my sister died before my mother, can I just
put the money into a building society as I don't
want things to get complicated? **"**

No. If you are holding money as a trustee for minors you must take
account of the obligations imposed by the Trustee Act 2000 as to the
suitability of the investments proposed and the need for diversification.
The Act also imposes a duty to review investments from time to time and
to take professional advice when carrying out that review.

" My mother left her house to me and my
three brothers. We all agreed to keep the
house and to let it out, but one of my
brothers now wants to sell the house. Can he
make us sell it? **"**

The short answer is yes. The sensible way forward is for the three of
you to agree a value with your brother and then to buy out his share.
As an alternative, you could put the house up for auction. If the price
is reasonable, the three of you can buy it and if the bidding gets too
high, you will get a quarter of the windfall.

OTHER PROBLEMS WITH WILLS

These points by no means cover all problems that can arise when administering a will, but here is information on events that most frequently occur.

> **❝ Missing beneficiaries can be tracked down through newspaper advertisements, the internet or a genealogist. With genealogists, try to employ him or her on a 'no-find no-fee' basis. ❞**

Bankrupt beneficiaries

If you suspect that a beneficiary is bankrupt or about to be made bankrupt, you should make further enquiries, including a search on form K16 at the Land Charges Registry (www.landregistry.gov.uk). Any payments due to a bankrupt must be made to his or her trustee in bankruptcy, who must produce an S.307 notice under the Insolvency Act 1986. Under these circumstances, consult a solicitor.

Missing beneficiaries

If you have to find beneficiaries, use what detective qualities you have. In addition to family networks and newspaper advertisements, you could use the internet to track down missing people. Genealogists can be engaged for intractable problems on a 'no-find no-fee' basis – check that their finding fee is a reasonable proportion of the sum involved.

If those steps get you nowhere, look at the possibility of insurance (don't forget to allow for interest on the bequest), failing which an application can be made to court to allow a distribution to be made on the assumption that the beneficiary has died without issue, or for the bequest to be paid into the court under the provisions of the Trustee Act 1925.

Problem executors or administrators

If it appears that a personal representative is unsuitable or is failing to carry out his or her duties, an application for removal can be made to the High Court. Before doing so, it is wise to ask the Probate Registrar or a solicitor with specific experience for advice.

Claims by ex-spouses or civil partners, dependants and family members

If there is an ex-spouse or civil partner to whom maintenance is still being paid following a divorce or separation, he or she is entitled to make a claim against the estate, so remember to take this possibility into account. The extent of the claim will depend upon the size of the estate and the other claimants. Similarly, a cohabitee or child of the deceased who considers the will to be unfair can make a claim against the estate under the provisions of the Inheritance (Provision for Family and Dependants) Act 1975. Under the Act, the adult claimant has to file a claim no later than six months after the grant of probate or letters of administration. If there is any risk of a claim being made, executors should limit any distribution made during that six-month period.

Having the right to claim does not mean that a person automatically wins the case if a claim is made, especially where the applicant has not been dependent on the deceased. Legal costs of the action are a matter for the court to decide. Such a person is not paid automatically by the estate, nor are the costs paid automatically from the estate.

❝ When the Court of Protection is involved, there are additional formalities to attend to with the court before the assets can come under your control. **❞**

Q *My sister died without making a will. She has no children but the man she used to see on a regular basis is now saying that he is entitled to claim a share of the estate because they were cohabiting before her death. Can he make such a claim?*

A The claim will have to be made under the Inheritance (Provision for Family and Dependants) Act 1975. Your sister's partner can make the claim, but the claim will not succeed unless he can establish the various grounds set out in the Act. You need to discuss this with your solicitor.

Court of Protection

If the affairs of the person who has died have been administered by the Court of Protection (in cases of mental illness, for example), there are formalities to go through with the court before the assets of the deceased can come under the control of the personal representatives.

This usually requires the 'Deputy' to file final accounts at the Court of Protection but, if all interested parties agree, that particular requirement can be waived.

The Deputy is the person who is appointed by the court to look after the financial affairs of people who cannot look after themselves, who are known as 'patients'.

For an outline of the rules of intestacy, see pages 11-12 and pages 143-4, which might help throw light on your particular case.

Foreign property

Generally speaking, if a deceased person owned property or land in another country, the laws there determine what happens to the property at death and may overrule what is said in the English or Welsh will. Seek advice from a solicitor with specific knowledge of the relevant law of the country involved. The Law Society can provide names of suitable solicitors.

Q *My sister has just died. She lived in Spain for the last ten years of her life in her own home. I think I have to go by Spanish law for the administration of her estate. Is this right?*
A If your sister had a foreign domicile (that is, her permanent home was in Spain and she intended to remain there), the law of the country of domicile applies to the administration of the estate. However, if your sister owned any property in England or Wales, you will need to seek a grant of probate to deal with it. Domicile is a tricky question for which you should consult a solicitor.

Caveats and citations

If you wish to prevent the issue of a grant of probate because you believe the will is invalid or that the applicant has no right to apply, you may file a caveat at the Probate Registry. This prevents probate being issued while the problem is resolved. If you simply want to know when probate is issued, you should make a standing search. If the caveat is challenged by a warning, that has the effect of commencing a probate action.

A citation is a formal request to the Probate Court to get someone to do something, such as where an executor will not apply for probate or administer the estate but will not renounce his or her appointment either.

> **!** Other probate disputes can end up in the Family or Chancery Divisions of the High Court. In either case, the proceedings will be costly and you will need to take advice. Neither court is DIY territory.

 For advice about buying a home overseas, see the *Which? Essential Guide* to *Buying Property Abroad*.

Wills and confirmation in Scotland

The legal details of making a will and seeking confirmation in Scotland are different to England and Wales. This chapter outlines such differences, with references to the main body of the book when the procedure remains the same.

Making your will

Advice on drafting wills in England and Wales applies equally to wills in Scotland. Use clear and precise language, and avoid technical terms and anything not strictly essential.

If there is ambiguity or a dispute about the meaning of a provision in a will that cannot be resolved by agreement, the matter may have to go to court, causing expense and delay. For this reason it is true to say that lawyers make more money from badly drawn-up homemade wills than they do from drafting them properly. Inheritance Tax (IHT) and its exemptions, including the 'seven-year rule' regarding lifetime gifts and gifts with reservation, apply in Scotland. In other ways, there are considerable differences in law, practice and procedure between the Scots law of wills and succession and the law as it applies in England and Wales.

LEGAL RIGHTS

Eligibility rules for wills in Scotland are the same as in England and Wales, with the exception that children aged 12 or over with their permanent home in Scotland can make valid wills there. In Scotland, you cannot disinherit your husband, wife or civil partner, or descendants completely. Whatever the will says, your husband, wife or civil partner has a right to a third of your '**moveable estate**' – that is, all your possessions except land and buildings. This fraction is increased to one-half if you do not leave any descendants. Similarly, the children among or between them have a right

Legal status of your entitlement

Not all items commonly regarded as property form part of a person's estate to be disposed of by a will. Further, such property outside the estate cannot be subject to a claim for legal rights. The most important examples are rights in a pension fund administered by trustees, whether established in connection with employment or personally, and certain types of insurance company bond.

If you own either of these types of pension fund or insurance bond, check the precise legal status of your entitlement and leave appropriate instructions with the trustees as a separate exercise from making your will.

o one-third or, if you are a widow/widower/surviving civil partner when you die, one-half of your moveable estate.

The executors appointed under the will have a duty to make sure that a person entitled to claim either does so or renounces his or her claim, and in theory a person claiming these rights, known as 'legal rights', simply has to inform the executors. In practice there must be cases where estates are wound up in ignorance of the position.

The surviving spouse, civil partner or children must choose between their legal rights and what they have been left in the will. They cannot have both.

Cohabitees now have rights in Scotland that are similar in nature to a spouse or civil partner's legal rights. See pages 173–4 for more details.

CHILDREN'S LEGAL CAPACITY

In accordance with the Age of Legal Capacity (Scotland) Act 1991, an individual of 16 or over has legal capacity for most practical purposes and is legally empowered to give a receipt for and obtain a transfer of money and property. The age of 'majority' remains 18 but this is of much less significance than in the past. There are two main consequences:

- A will should refer to an age expressly – 'when she is 18' rather than 'when she comes of age' or 'when she attains the age of majority'.
- Many people feel that 16 is too young for a person to be placed in charge of large sums of money. If you prefer the legatee not to acquire control of the legacy until he or she is, say, 21 or 25, you must set up a trust with special provisions (see pages 35–6) to achieve this result. It is not enough just to provide that payment should be delayed.
- If a will appoints guardians and does not say when the appointment ends (typically at the age of 16), then the appointment will continue until the age of 18 years.

A will that refers to children is interpreted to include natural and adopted children but not, unless specifically mentioned, stepchildren. Scots law presumes that, if a child is born to you after you have made a will, you would wish to make a new will including the addition to your family. Your existing will may do this by a provision in favour of 'all my children' but, if it does not, or where the children to benefit are named, the child born later can apply to the court for the will to be set aside. In these circumstances, the court will do so unless it is satisfied that your real intention was to exclude the child.

66 In Scotland, an individual of 16 or over no longer has a guardian and has legal capacity for most practical purposes. 99

An example of a will made in Scotland

The will given here contains elements that are pertinent to Scottish law. Notes are given at the end of the will (opposite).

I, Mrs JEANNIE SCOTT or DEANS, residing at 999 Waverley Street, Glasgow G43 9ZZ for the settlement of my affairs after my death REVOKE all former testamentary writings made by me and declare this to be my last Will: That is to say I nominate my sister Griselda Scott and Robert Burns, residing at The Cottage, Alloway, Ayrshire and the survivor to be my Executors: And I convey to my Executors the whole estate, heritable and moveable, real and personal which shall belong to me at the time of my death: BUT THAT IN TRUST for the following purposes:-

FIRST To pay my debts and funeral expenses and the expenses of winding up my estate:

SECOND To give effect to any directions contained in any writings signed by me however informal and that free of tax and without interest unless otherwise stated:

THIRD To pay as soon as convenient free of tax but without interest the following cash legacies namely (one) to John Lennon, residing at Central Park, New York the sum of One hundred Pounds and (two) to The Society for the Preservation of Ancient Solicitors the sum of Fifty Pounds (declaring that the receipt of their Treasurer will be a sufficient discharge to my Executors):

FOURTH To deliver to my friend Victor Meldrew, residing care of the BBC free of tax as his own absolute property my oil painting entitled 'The Wreck of the Hesperus':

FIFTH To allow my sister Griselda Scott the free use and enjoyment of my dwellinghouse at 999 Waverley Street aforesaid together with the whole household furniture, furnishings and contents thereof for as long as she may require it subject to a maximum period of two years from my date of death subject to her paying all ordinary maintenance costs, the rates and taxes falling on an owner or occupier in respect thereof and the cost of insurance for reinstatement value against normal risks: AND

SIXTH To pay, convey and make over the residue of my said estate to my cousins equally among them and the survivors of them all as their respective own absolute property, declaring that the children of any of them who shall predecease me shall take, equally among them if more than one, the share which their parent would have taken had he or she survived me:

IN WITNESS WHEREOF I have subscribed these presents at Glasgow on 1 April 2007 before this witness:-

Signature of Witness

Full Name of Witness   Douglas J McLean

Address of Witness   18 Dechmond Street, Parkhead, Glasgow
                            G43 9LK

Notes

- In Scotland, married women traditionally retained their maiden name and this is often reflected in legal documents, but it is not necessary to show both names. Hence 'Scott' is the deceased's maiden name and 'Deans' not an alias but her married name. 'Jeannie' is probably not the deceased's correct birth certificate name, but is in order in Scotland if this was how she was known.

- Various persons are named but their addresses are not given. This is in order only where the person is clearly identified. It is better to give addresses.

- The informal writings clause is very convenient to deal with small items. It is acceptable in Scotland.

- The cash legacies are unrealistically small. Persons making wills should carefully assess the value of their estate and make a reasonable provision for legatees, who are often close friends.

- The provision regarding the house illustrates that clear instructions can be given in a will, even though they may not be bequests of a traditional type.

- Every will should contain a bequest of residue to avoid partial intestacy.

- The signing docquet is in accordance with current law and practice. It is no longer necessary in Scotland for a witness's occupation to be stated.

DEATH OF BENEFICIARY

A person has to survive the deceased by only an instant in order to inherit. Where it cannot be known who died first, the younger is deemed to have survived the older, except in the case of a husband and wife, where simultaneous deaths are assumed. These rules can have unintended consequences so, as in England or Wales, it is normal to state a specific period of survivorship of, say, 14 or 30 days. This also has tax benefits, because if, say, a husband survives his wife by only a couple of days, their estates would be combined, which can increase the overall tax bill. However, new tax rules allowing Inheritance Tax nil-rate bands to be transferred tetween spouses or civil partners may reduce the overall tax impact, depending on individual circumstances.

If the person to whom you leave the legacy dies before you and is not your child, the legacy lapses, so that it falls into the residue of your estate. If the bequest was of a share of residue, the result can be complicated. Sometimes the lapsed share goes to the other named beneficiaries, sometimes there is a partial intestacy. The best solution is for the will to spell out what should happen if a beneficiary predeceases the testator.

WHO SHOULD BE THE EXECUTORS?

All executors nominated in the will who survive the deceased are entitled to act, and unless they decline, they are 'confirmed' – that is, officially approved by the sheriff court to administer the will In all but the simplest estates, it is probably better to have two executors to guard against a sole executor acting incorrectly or becoming incapacitated or dying before completing the administration. There is no rule preventing a beneficiary from being an executor and in many cases, for example wills between husband and wife, this is the best course.

SIGNING THE WILL

New rules introduced in Scotland relate to the validity of wills dated on or after 1 August 1995. Under these new rules, a will that complies with certain simple requirements (listed below) is now regarded as 'self-proving'. Unless it is challenged – for example, because the deceased did not sign it – the will is presumed to be valid. A will that does not comply has to be proved by a petition to the court, which involves expense and may not succeed. Accordingly, all wills should now meet the following formal requirements for self-proving status.

- The document must be signed by the testator at the end.
- If the document consists of more than one sheet, it must be signed on each sheet.

❝ Under new rules, a will that complies with certain simple requirements is seen as 'self-proving'. ❞

- **The signature must be attested** by one 'competent' witness, who must sign immediately after the testator signs to acknowledge his or her signature. The witness's name and address should appear in the text of the document or in a 'testing' clause added at the end. This information need not be written by the witness and can be added after the event.
- **Blind people may sign their own wills.** Alternatively, they (and other people who cannot write) may use another method. This involves a solicitor, advocate, sheriff clerk or justice of the peace reading the will to the testator and signing it after receiving the testator's authority to do so. The signature is then witnessed as above.

Witnesses

Certain people are not competent to act as witnesses, mainly children below the age of 16, blind people (as they cannot see the testator signing) and those suffering from mental incapacity. It is not good practice for a person with an interest (such as a beneficiary) to sign, as this may become material if the will is later challenged. Similarly, a person may, but should not, act as a witness to his or her spouse or civil partner's signature.

❝ Blind people may sign their own wills or an official can read it to the testator and then sign it following the testator's authority to do so. ❞

STORING THE WILL

There is no official depository in Scotland where your will can be kept while you are alive. Because of this it sometimes happens that estates are dealt with wrongly on the basis that there is no will, or on the basis of an out-of-date will that has been revoked by a later one. It is not really safe to keep the will at home, nor is it sensible to leave it in a bank, because an annual charge will be made and when the time comes for it to be referred to, it will be difficult for the family to get access to it quickly. Wherever it is, leave a note in your personal papers telling your executors how to find it. Most solicitors provide safe storage for a will, free of charge.

After a person has died, his or her will is normally produced to the sheriff clerk in connection with an application for confirmation (the Scottish term used to describe both the English terms 'probate' (proof of a will) and 'letters of administration' (power to wind up where there is no will)). The clerk keeps a copy in the court books, where it can be inspected by members of the public. The executor can also lodge the will in the Registers of Scotland in Edinburgh.

REVOKING A WILL

As in England, a will should contain a clause revoking all former wills. This ensures that the distribution of the estate is regulated by the most recent document. A will is also revoked if it is destroyed on your instructions, even if you are not present to see it done.

In Scotland, unlike England, a person's will is not automatically revoked by his or her subsequent marriage. Unless you make a new will, your spouse or civil partner can only inherit if they claim legal rights (see pages 156–7). Similarly, bequests to a husband or wife are not automatically invalidated by subsequent divorce or separation, and bequests to a civil partner are not automatically invalidated by dissolution of the partnership. So, if a marriage or civil partnership breaks down, it is better to put the matter beyond doubt by making a new will without delay.

❝ Unless you make a new will following revocation, your spouse or civil partner can only inherit if they claim legal rights. ❞

CO-OWNERSHIP OF MONEY AND PROPERTY

Where money is contained in a joint bank or building society account, it is not necessarily owned in equal shares. There are two main types of joint account. The first requires both the account holders to sign cheques. The second, which is more common, is called an 'either or survivor account'. In this case, either holder can sign cheques while both are alive. On the death of the first holder, the survivor can continue to sign cheques. This type of account, however, regulates only the entitlement of the holder to withdraw and the bank to pay money; it does not determine who owns it. Ownership depends on who put money into the account and their intentions in doing so. Where only one holder put money in and made the account joint so that the other could also sign cheques, the money remains the property of the contributing holder. On the other hand, if the intention was to pool resources, each holder has a half-share of the balance. The law assumes pooling resources was not intended, so this has to be proved.

Where both holders contributed, the balance is divided according to the contributions that each party made. If this is difficult to prove, the balance is divided equally.

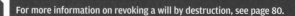

For more information on revoking a will by destruction, see page 80.

These rules also apply to joint accounts held by married couples. It is perhaps more likely in the case of a husband and wife that their intention was to pool resources, but the presumption against pooling still applies, except in the case of 'housekeeping' accounts, which are shared equally unless the couple specifies otherwise.

Where a house is held in common ownership without a survivorship provision (called a 'destination'), each owner's share forms part of his or her estate on death and is dealt with either by the will or the rules of intestacy. The share each owner possesses – usually equal – is stated in the title deed to the property.

A survivorship destination usually transfers the share of the first to die to the survivor. In some circumstances, depending on the wording of the title deed, you cannot change the destination. If, however, you are free to revoke it, you must do so expressly in your will.

When a marriage breaks down and either the husband or wife is taking over complete ownership, both must sign the transfer documents. Similar rules apply to civil partners. This branch of law is complicated and you are best advised to get expert help.

❝ Where a house is held in common ownership without a survivorship provision, each owner's share forms part of his or her estate on death. ❞

Administering the estate

In Scotland, the persons legally responsible for dealing with an estate are the executors. Unless a will provides otherwise, they are not entitled to be paid for their services but, if they seek help, professional fees are chargeable to the estate.

Only attempt the administrative work yourself if you are confident you have the necessary administrative and financial ability. If you don't, leave it to a competent professional person.

APPOINTMENT AND CONFIRMATION OF EXECUTORS

Executors appointed by your will are called **executors-nominate**. For a person who dies intestate, the court appoints an '**executor-dative**'. In this case, a member of the family, often the surviving spouse or civil partner, normally (except for small estates, whose value before deduction of debts does not exceed £30,000) has to petition the court in the place where the deceased was domiciled for appointment as executor-dative. Such petitions are best put in the hands of a solicitor. The court normally handles a petition within two weeks of its arrival.

All executors have to be officially 'confirmed' by the sheriff court before they can start collecting in the estate. However, confirmation of assets is not always needed. The rules for payments of smaller balances by organisations such as National Savings & Investments are the same in Scotland as in England and Wales. If the only item in the estate is a bank account, it is worth asking the bank for details of its own small estates procedure. Most will pay up to about £10,000–£15,000 against a formal receipt and indemnity. Confirmation is also unnecessary in the case of joint property where title is subject to a survivorship destination. On death, the deceased's share of the property passes to the other automatically, bypassing the executor.

If confirmation is required for even one item, all assets (cash, personal effects,

❝All executors have to be officially 'confirmed' by the sheriff court before they can start collecting the estate. ❞

Declining to be an administrator in Scotland

If an executor-nominate does not wish to act, he or she can decline to be confirmed. A simple signed statement to that effect is all that is needed. You cannot decline to be an executor-nominate but still reserve the right to apply later. If a sole executor-nominate declines, the family may have to apply to the court for another executor to be appointed.

In such a case, it is always quicker and cheaper for the nominated executor to bring someone else in as co-executor and then decline, leaving the co-executor to be confirmed and act alone.

furniture, car and similar items) have to be entered in an inventory for confirmation. They do not need to be professionally valued, however, and may be valued by the executor. Unless the title to the property contains a survivorship destination (when the share is disclosed for tax purposes only), the deceased's share of joint property must also be confirmed.

Jargon buster

'Confirmation' The Scottish term used to describe both the English terms 'probate' and 'letters of administration'

Executor-dative An administrator appointed by the court for a person who dies intestate

Executor-nominate The Scottish term for the English term 'executor'

❝All assets do not need to be professionally valued before being entered in an inventory for confirmation. They can be perfectly well valued by the executor.❞

 Useful websites for executors in Scotland include: www.hmrc.gov.uk/inheritancetax (HM Revenue & Customs Capital Taxes (Scotland)), www.ros.gov.uk (Registers of Scotland) and www.scotcourts.gov.uk (Sheriff Clerks' Office).

ADMINISTRATOR OF AN INTESTATE ESTATE IN SCOTLAND

If you are an executor-dative appointed by the court, you are required to supply a guarantee that you will carry out your duties as executor properly before confirmation is issued. This guarantee is called a 'bond of caution' (pronounced 'kayshun') and is usually provided by an insurance company.

In recent years, the insurance companies have become more difficult about issuing these bonds and the premiums quoted can be quite high. This is an area where almost certainly an executor will require professional help, as the insurers are reluctant to issue bonds to inexperienced executors. Instead of an insurance company, you can, in theory, have an individual as a cautioner but the court would need to be satisfied that, if called upon to do so, the individual is able to pay the sum due. In practice this course is not an option.

Losses caused by the negligence or fraud of an executor are made good by the cautioner in the first instance, with the cautioner then seeking to recover the money from the executor personally.

A bond of caution is not required if you are a surviving spouse or civil partner and you inherit the estate by virtue of your prior rights (see pages 176–8).

FIRST FORMALITIES FOR EXECUTORS

Executors, whether nominated in the will or appointed by the court, have limited powers before confirmation. In this period, they should confine themselves to safeguarding and investigating the estate. They should not hand over any items to beneficiaries. Any person who interferes with the deceased's property may be held personally liable for all the deceased's debts, however large. This liability of confirmed executors for debts is limited to the overall value of the estate, provided they acted prudently and within their legal authority before confirmation.

❝ Insurance companies are not always easy to deal with on the subject of issuing a bond of caution and the premiums can be quite high. ❞

 For more information about intestate succession in Scotland, see pages 173-8.

OBTAINING CONFIRMATION FORMS

To apply for confirmation, you need to fill in an inventory of the deceased's estate: **form C1**. You can download this from www.hmrc.gov.uk/cto/forms/c1_2_lined. pdf. In addition, you need **form C5** and notes to help you fill in forms C1 and C5 (**form C3**). You may also need **form C2**, which is a continuation sheet for the inventory.

● All forms can be downloaded from the HM Revenue & Customs (HMRC) website (www.hmrc.gov.uk). It is possible to fill them in and return them online.

 If an executor discovers that the estate is insolvent, he or she should not continue with the administration but should take advice immediately from an insolvency adviser or from a Citizens Advice Bureau, an accountant or a solicitor. It may be necessary to petition the court immediately for a trustee to be appointed to administer the estate – otherwise, the executor may become personally liable for the debts.

● Also, printed copies can be obtained from the Commissary Department of the Sheriff Clerks' Office (www.scotcourts.gov.uk). There are no special forms for lay applicants.

Certain estates fall within an 'excepted estate' category (see box, overleaf). If the estate you are administering doesn't fall into this category, you must also fill in IHT400 (see page 123).

If it is likely that there is IHT to pay, or if the declarations contained in form C5 cannot be made, because, for example, gifts have been made, HMRC requires a return on form IHT400. Normally a return on this form is required if the estate exceeds the tax threshold for that year (£325,000 in 2009–10). If you are applying before 6 August in any year, the requirement is based on the previous year's threshold (£312,000 in 2008–9).

❝ All forms can be downloaded from the HM Revenue & Customs website. ❞

IHT due by the executors must be paid before confirmation is sought. Because the estate's funds are, in effect, frozen at this stage, the executors must ask a bank for temporary overdraft facilities to pay the tax. In some cases, HM Revenue & Customs is able to transfer funds from the deceased's bank directly (see also pages 127–8).

Completing form C1

Once you have all the information regarding the valuation of the assets in the estate and the deceased's debts (see pages 106–22), you are ready to fill in form C1 for obtaining confirmation. When there is more than one executor, one of them applies on behalf of all. If there is disagreement among the persons entitled to apply, the Sheriff can be asked to make a ruling. An executor appointed by the will who does not wish to act must sign a statement to this effect. This accompanies the application for confirmation.

You first fill in details of the deceased and the appointment of executors. You have to make formal statements and complete and sign a declaration. Any document referred to, such as the will, should be marked up as relating to the declaration and signed. List all the estate in the United Kingdom and moveable estate abroad asset by asset together with their value. This ensures that everyone holding an asset hands it over. Assets should be listed in the following order:

- Heritable estate (that is, land or buildings) in Scotland. A typical example is the deceased's house if he or she was sole or part-owner. While the postal address of a house is normally a good enough description, for land you need to use the formal wording in the title deeds. Include the Title Number if the property is registered in the Land Register of Scotland. Do not include here property whose title contains a survivorship destination.
- Moveable estate in Scotland. This includes cash, furniture and personal effects, car, bank or building society accounts where the branch is in Scotland, National Savings &

Excepted estates

An excepted estate is an estate where no IHT is due and a full IHT account is not required. From 6 April 2004 there are three types of excepted estate:

- Low-value estate
- Exempt estates
- Foreign domiciliaries

For more information on these types of estate, go to www.hmrc.gov.uk/cto/forms/c3-2006-2.pdf. See also the relevant notes in form C3.

❝On form C1 first fill in the details of the deceased and the executors, completing and signing a declaration of intent. ❞

Investments and government stock, shares in Scottish companies, income tax refunds, arrears of pay or pension and all other debts due to the deceased.

- **Real and personal estate in England and Wales.** Real estate (land or buildings) is put first. Personal estate is other types of property, such as shares in English companies.
- **Real and personal estate in Northern Ireland.** As for England and Wales.
- **Real estate outside the United Kingdom.** This should be listed in a separate will made in the country concerned.
- **Moveable estate outside the UK,** such as shares in foreign companies.

Summarise the value of the estate under the above headings, and you then have the total amount for confirmation. There is a set way in which the summary is prepared for the Sheriff Clerk.

Lodging the form

Post or deliver the form to the sheriff court that is nearest where the deceased was domiciled at the time of death. If you are in any doubt, ask your local sheriff court to advise you. At the same time as you lodge the will, you pay the fee for confirmation. For estates up to £5,000 there is no fee; for estates larger than £5,000 the fee is £195. Please note that these fees are liable to be increased without warning.

For an estate with a range of assets, ask for certificates of confirmation for individual items of estate. These cost £5 each if ordered when you apply for confirmation. You can collect the assets simultaneously, using the appropriate certificate of confirmation as evidence of your right to demand and receive them.

❝Ensure you summarise the value of the estate in the appropriate way.❞

After a week or so, if everything is in order, the confirmation is sent to you by post and the will is returned, the court keeping a copy for its records. The confirmation itself is a photocopy of parts of the form you lodged showing details of the deceased, the executors and all the assets of the estate in the United Kingdom together with a page in which the sheriff court 'in Her Majesty's name and authority approves of and confirms' the named executor(s) and 'gives and commits to the said executor(s) full power' in relation to the estate.

To find a full list of the Scottish courts, go to www.scotcourts.gov.uk/locations /index.asp, which gives addresses and contact names together with information on getting to the court, if necessary.

PROCEDURE FOR SMALL ESTATES

To reduce the expense of obtaining confirmation, special procedures apply to small estates, which, before deduction of debts, have a gross value of less than £30,000. For a small estate with no will, you do not have to petition the court for appointment of an executor, and the necessary forms are completed for you by the staff at the sheriff court. Whether or not a will exists, you apply to any convenient sheriff court by post or in person. You take (or send) to the court:

- A list of all assets and their values
- A list of debts (including the funeral account)
- The deceased's full name and address, date of birth and date and place of death
- The will, if there is one.

The sheriff clerk then prepares the

❝ For small estates, confirmation is sent to you by post or to the executor-dative appointed by the court a few days after the appropriate form has been signed. ❞

appropriate form for you to sign then and there or to return in a few days' time. The fee for confirmation is payable on signing the form. No fee is charged if the estate is below £5,000. Above that figure, the fee is currently £195. A few days after you have signed the form, confirmation is sent to you by post or to the executor-dative appointed by the court. The will is returned, with the court keeping a copy for its records.

PAYING DEBTS

Now that you are confirmed as executor, you first pay the deceased's debts. Some of these may be secured against specific assets, for example a building society loan where the building society has a security on the deceased's home or an overdraft for which the bank holds a life policy as security. Other debts, such as medical and funeral expenses, the cost of obtaining confirmation, tax bills and ordinary accounts, can be paid as soon as it is clear that there are sufficient funds. If funds seem insufficient, the executors must take immediate advice.

Ordinary creditors are expected to claim within a reasonable period, usually taken to be within six months of the deceased's death. It is now not very common to advertise for claims in the press, but whether or not to do so depends on the circumstances. If the

The Department of Work and Pensions (DWP) is at website www.dwp.gov.uk; to contact the benefit fraud department telephone: 0800 854 440 (free).

170

deceased had complicated or confused business affairs, it would be advisable to advertise. After six months from the date of death or such longer period as executors decide (there is no written rule about this and practice varies among law firms), executors can pay all known creditors and distribute the balance of the estate to the beneficiaries.

Creditors who claim later are paid if the executors still have the estate in their hands. Executors who have no estate left do not have to pay such creditors out of their own pockets unless it can be claimed they should have known of their existence.

Problems can arise if the deceased was claiming social security benefits to which he or she was not entitled. The Department of Work and Pensions checks inventories lodged at court and is entitled to claim back any overpayment from an estate. If this is a possibility, it is prudent to send the department an enquiry (see box, below opposite).

> **❝ If a child is under 16, he or she cannot legally decide whether to renounce or claim legal rights. ❞**

LEGAL RIGHTS

You must not forget about legal rights – see page 156. You should write to every person who could claim, telling them how much their legal rights are worth and suggesting they take legal advice before deciding what to do.

Children can present a particular problem. If they are under 16, they cannot legally decide whether to renounce or claim and, since the surviving spouse or civil partner has a conflicting interest, he or she cannot renounce on their behalf as guardian. Children aged 16 and 17 can renounce but the court should be asked to ratify their decision. Unless this happens, children can apply to the court later if they feel they renounced wrongly.

Where the legal rights are under £5,000, the executors may hand over the money to the surviving parent (or guardian), who should invest it for the children. Alternatively, the executors may open a building society account or buy National Savings & Investments certificates in the child's name and hand over the passbook or certificates to the parent. A parent (or guardian) who misappropriates the money may be sued for its return.

For sums over £20,000, the executors should contact the Office of the Accountant of Court (see box, below).

To find out more about National Savings & Investments certificates, go to www.nsandi.com/products/index.jsp. The website for the Office of the Accountant of Court is at www.scotcourts.gov.uk/session/accountant.asp.

The Accountant of Court is a government official based in Edinburgh who, after considering the circumstances, decides how the money is to be best managed. The options are:

- A court-appointed manager (for large sums only)
- The Accountant of Court to be manager
- The parent (or guardian) to be manager but supervised by the Accountant of Court.

TRANSFER OF THE HOUSE

If the title deed contained a survivorship destination, the executor is not involved in transferring the house of the person who died. The deceased's share of the house is automatically transferred to the surviving co-owner. In other cases, the house must be transferred to a beneficiary under the will or the rules of intestacy (see pages 11–12).

The procedure for this involves, in simple cases, the preparation of a form of transfer attached to the confirmation and, in more complicated cases, a 'disposition', which is a formal conveyancing document. The documents are lodged in the public registers in Edinburgh. If the titles are already registered, the procedures are different from unregistered property. In either case, this work should be done by a solicitor. At the same time as the title is transferred, and if money is available, any building society loan can be discharged. Otherwise, arrangements need to be made for the loan to continue under the new owner's name or for a new loan.

PAYING LEGACIES

Wills usually provide that no interest is due on a legacy but that it is clear of tax. However, the actual wording must be checked. Otherwise interest at an appropriate rate can be claimed if the executor has delayed unreasonably in paying out. The executor should take care to get a receipt.

SETTLING THE RESIDUE

Once the executor has paid the debts and legacies and complied with bequests and any other instructions, the remainder of the estate, the residue, can be divided according to the will. As in England and Wales, the executor should provide the beneficiaries with a draft set of accounts for approval before settling with them. Payment should be made against receipts from them.

Entitlement on intestacy

A person who dies without leaving a will is said to die intestate. Where there is a will dealing with only part of the estate, the result is described as partial intestacy.

For example, a person may leave a will dealing with his or her house, furniture and savings, but overlook, say, his or her life policies. On his or her death the house, furniture and savings are distributed in accordance with the will, and the remainder of the estate by application of the intestacy rules. In general, total or partial intestacy is to be avoided, but there may be rare occasions when a person wishes to defeat legal rights claims and uses intestacy deliberately.

In certain circumstances, you can disinherit your children by dying without a will. Provided your estate is not too

valuable, your surviving spouse or civil partner's rights to the house, furniture and cash can swallow up the whole estate, leaving nothing for the children. If you had made a will that left everything to your husband or wife, your children could claim their legal rights to one-third of your moveable estate.

The rules of intestacy are set out in the Succession (Scotland) Act 1964 and represent what Parliament then considered to be a reasonable distribution for the average family. Since then, society has changed greatly and the Family Law (Scotland) Act 2006 makes changes to the law to try to take some account of modern lifestyles. For example, cohabitees who are not married to each other (opposite sex relationships) or who are not in civil partnership with each other (same sex relationships), now have a right to apply to the sheriff court for a discretionary financial provision from the estate of their deceased partner, if intestate. This right must be exercised

"The rules of intestacy are set out in the Succession (Scotland) Act 1964."

The deceased may not necessarily have died intestate. If you aren't sure, see pages 84–6, which outlines where a will can be stored. These would be your first ports of call if searching for an extant will.

within six months of the deceased's death and can be either an award of a capital sum or of a transfer of property. A number of factors have to be taken into account by the court when determining what level of award is appropriate, but a surviving cohabitant will never be better off than if the cohabitant had been married to or in civil partnership with the deceased. If the deceased left a will, then a surviving cohabitant's right to make a claim in the sheriff court is defeated.

Under the 1964 Act as amended, the law does not discriminate between children born in or out of marriage or between natural or adopted children. A divorced person or a former civil partner cannot inherit from his or her ex-spouse or ex-civil partner and, where a person with a child later marries or enters into civil partnership, the child cannot inherit from his or her step-parent.

Generally, the division on intestacy depends on the size of the estate, the nature of the assets and which relatives survive. The more straightforward case of a single or widowed person's estate is dealt with first.

❝ The division on intestacy depends on the size of the estate, the nature of the assets and which relatives survive. ❞

DECEASED LEAVES NO SURVIVING SPOUSE OR CIVIL PARTNER

When a person dies without leaving a surviving spouse or civil partner, the estate passes to the surviving relatives in the following order:

- Descendants (children, grandchildren and so on)
- Brothers, sisters (and their descendants) and parents
- Uncles and aunts (and their descendants)
- Grandparents
- Great-uncles and great-aunts (and their descendants)
- Great-grandparents,

and so on until a relative is found to inherit. Different rules apply to different categories of surviving relatives.

Children

The children share the estate equally among them, with descendants of a child who died before the deceased generally taking that child's share. However, if all the children are dead, the grandchildren share the estate equally, the descendants of a deceased grandchild taking the share that grandchild would have taken had he or she survived.

Brothers, sisters and parents

Where the deceased leaves no surviving children and no surviving parents, his or her brothers and sisters share the estate equally among them, with the descendants of a brother or sister who died before the deceased generally taking his or her share. However, if all the brothers and sisters are dead, their children (the deceased's nephews or nieces) share the estate equally among them, the descendants of a dead nephew or niece taking the share he or she would have taken. A child jointly adopted by a couple is treated as a full brother or sister of any other child they adopt or of any child of their marriage. Half-brothers and half-sisters get a share only if there are no full brothers or sisters or their descendants.

Where the deceased leaves no surviving brothers or sisters (or their descendants) but leaves both parents, they inherit the estate equally. If only one parent survives, he or she inherits the entire estate.

Where there are both brothers and sisters (or their descendants) and a parent or parents left, the estate is divided into two. One half goes to each group.

66 **When the deceased leaves no surviving children and no surviving parents, his or her brothers and sisters share the estate equally.** 99

Uncles and aunts

Next in line are brothers and sisters of the deceased's parents – his or her uncles and aunts. The uncles and aunts share the estate equally among them, with the descendants of an uncle or aunt who died before the deceased generally taking his or her share. However, if all the uncles and aunts are dead, their children (the deceased's cousins) share the estate equally between them, the descendants of a dead cousin taking the share that cousin would have taken.

Grandparents

Next in line are the deceased's grandparents. They share the estate among them or, if there is only one alive, he or she inherits the entire estate.

Remoter relatives

After grandparents come great-uncles and great-aunts or their descendants (namely second cousins and second cousins once removed). The further the search extends for someone to inherit, the more complex the inheritance becomes.

The Crown

If, when a person dies and the debts and funeral expenses have been paid but no surviving relatives have been traced, the estate goes to the Crown's formal representative, the Queen's and Lord Treasurer's Remembrancer. This official advertises for claimants in local newspapers. If no relative claims the estate, the Crown may be prepared to make gifts from the estate to people with a moral but no legal claim to the estate, such as a cohabiting partner or a neighbour who gave substantial help to the deceased without payment. Further, if a relative turns up after an estate has been paid over to the Crown, he or she should be able to claim the inheritance.

> ❝ The law provides first for the surviving spouse or civil partner to receive 'prior rights'. Next come the 'legal rights' of the surviving spouse or civil partner and any children. ❞

DECEASED LEAVES A SURVIVING SPOUSE OR CIVIL PARTNER

Briefly, the law provides first for the surviving spouse or civil partner to receive 'prior rights' (see box, below). Next come the 'legal rights' of the surviving spouse or civil partner and any children. The remainder of the estate (if any) is taken by the nearest relatives.

Prior rights: the house

The surviving spouse or civil partner is entitled to the house owned by the deceased, provided:

- It is situated in Scotland
- He or she was ordinarily resident in the house at the date of the deceased's death
- It is not worth more than £300,000.

Where the deceased owned a share of the house, the surviving spouse or civil partner gets that share, provided it is worth less than £300,000 and the other conditions are satisfied. The surviving spouse or civil partner gets £300,000 instead of the house or share of the house if either is worth more than £300,000. If the house is part of a larger property run as a business and it would be disadvantageous to separate the house, the surviving spouse or civil partner gets the value (up to £300,000) instead of the house. This situation

Jargon buster

Prior rights Rights to the house, its furnishings and a cash sum. Except in the case of larger estates, where intestacy is rare, prior rights often mean that the surviving spouse or civil partner inherits the entire estate. The financial figures given here are reviewed from time to time and as at 2009 have not been changed since 2005

ould particularly arise with a farm and farmhouse.

Where the house has a loan secured on it, the surviving spouse or civil partner receives only the net value – the value of the house less the outstanding balance of the loan. This is so even if the deceased had a life policy to pay off the loan on death.

Prior rights: the furnishings

The surviving spouse or civil partner is entitled to up to £24,000 of furnishings owned by the deceased. These need not be in a home owned by the deceased. For example, the couple's house may have been rented or belong to the surviving spouse or civil partner already. Where the deceased's furnishings are worth more than £24,000, the surviving spouse or civil partner selects items to his value.

Prior rights: cash sum

If the deceased left no children or other descendants, the surviving spouse or civil partner gets up to £75,000, but only up to £42,000 otherwise.

Legal rights

These come into play after prior rights have been taken. If there are surviving children, the surviving spouse or civil partner is entitled to one-third of the remaining net moveable estate (estate other than land and buildings). The children share another third among them. If there are no surviving children or other descendants, the surviving spouse or civil partner's fraction is increased to one-half.

Calculating the size of the remaining net moveable estate in order to work out legal rights is complicated.

- **Debts and liabilities of the estate** must be set against either land and buildings (the heritable estate) or the moveable estate.
- **While a loan secured over the house** is a debt against the heritable estate and the funeral account and ordinary bills are debts against the moveable estate, IHT and administration expenses are apportioned between the heritable and moveable estates depending on their respective values.

❝ With prior rights comprising rights to a house, its furnishings and a cash sum, the surviving spouse or civil partner often inherits the entire estate. ❞

- **Where the deceased owned heritable estate apart from the house,** the prior rights cash sum of £75,000 (or, where there are children, £42,000) is treated as having been taken partly from the other heritable estate and partly from the moveable estate.

Children normally share the money representing their legal rights equally. Where one of the children dies before the deceased, leaving children, these children – the deceased's grandchildren – share the dead child's share. Where all the children have died, all the grandchildren share equally. A child who renounces his or her legal rights while the deceased is alive does not share, and this will normally preclude a later claim by his or her descendants. A child's share can also be affected if the deceased gives him or her a substantial lifetime gift on marriage, for example, or to provide long-term income.

The remainder of the estate

After prior and legal rights have been met, any remainder of the estate goes to the deceased's nearest relatives. The order is children, grandchildren and remoter descendants, then brothers, sisters (or their descendants) and parents. The rules for division between these relatives are the same as where the deceased left no surviving spouse or civil partner (see pages 174–6). If the deceased leaves no surviving relatives in the above categories, the surviving spouse or civil partner inherits the entire estate.

LAW REFORM

The Scottish Law Commission issued a report in April 2009 recommending far reaching reforms to the law of succession in Scotland, including the law of intestacy. The report will only become law if the Scottish Parliament decides to accept any of the detailed proposals made by the Scottish Law Commission. It could be some time before any changes are made. In the meantime, the rules set out here, which largely come from the Succession (Scotland) Act 1964, still apply.

❝ After prior and legal rights have been met, any remainder of the estate goes to the deceased's nearest relatives in a pre-determined order. ❞

Wills and probate in Northern Ireland

The law on wills and probate in Northern Ireland is similar to that in England and Wales. In fact, the law relating to wills is almost identical, following legislation passed on 1 January 1995. However, the laws for probate vary a little and it is these differences that are covered here.

10

The will and probate

One major difference between England and Wales and Northern Ireland has been created by the Wills and Administration Proceedings (Northern Ireland) Order 1994 legislation.

In Northern Ireland, provided the will is actually signed after 1 January 1995, a married minor or minors who have been married can now make a valid will. However, it is not possible for a married minor in England or Wales to make a valid will. The Administration of Estates Act 1925 (see page 8) does not apply in Northern Ireland. The equivalent legislation is the Administration of Estates Act (Northern Ireland) 1955. Likewise, the Trustee Act 2000 does not apply in Northern Ireland. However, the Trustee Act (NI) 2001, which is very similar to the Trustee Act 2000, came into force on 29 July 2002.

After someone dies and probate has been obtained, anyone can apply to see it or obtain a copy of it at the Probate Office, Royal Courts of Justice (see box, below). If it is more than five years since the grant was obtained, application should be made to the Public Record Office of Northern Ireland (see also box, below).

HOW NORTHERN IRELAND DIFFERS

Use the basic information already given for England and Wales on pages 87–130, but take into account the special conditions in Northern Ireland relating to the issues discussed below.

Death of husband and wife or civil partner

In Northern Ireland, the common-law presumption of simultaneous deaths in cases where it is not certain who died first still applies. For this reason it is often desirable to insert an express

❝ There is no recommended scale of fees for solicitors in Northern Ireland, but there are guidelines for everyone to follow. ❞

 The website for the Royal Courts of Justice is www.courtsni.gov.uk, or to get in touch with the Public Record Office of Northern Ireland, go to www.proni.gov.uk.

provision in the will that one spouse or civil partner is to benefit under the other's will only if he or she survives the testator by a fixed period, usually 30 days (see pages 56–7).

Executor not wishing to act

Only if the executor resides outside Northern Ireland or resides in Northern Ireland but the Master is satisfied by affidavit (see page 147) that it is desirable for a grant to be made to his attorney can a person named as an executor in a will appoint an attorney. So, when you make your will, make sure that your nominated executors are willing and likely to be able to serve.

❝ Different offices need to be applied to for probate forms depending on where the deceased resided. ❞

Advertising for creditors and beneficiaries

The special procedure for formally advertising for creditors and beneficiaries in Northern Ireland requires both an advertisement in the *Belfast Gazette* and an advertisement twice in each of any two daily newspapers printed and published in Northern Ireland. If the assets include land, the advertisements should be in the *Belfast Gazette* and in any two newspapers circulating in the district where the land is situated.

The advertisements in the papers should require any interested parties to send in particulars of their claim within a set period of time, which is not to be less than two months, and which will run from the date of publication of the last notice.

Applying for probate forms

Personal applications for probate forms should be made to the Probate and Matrimonial Office, Royal Courts of Justice in Belfast, or the District Probate Registry in Londonderry.

- If the deceased had a fixed place of abode within the counties of Fermanagh, Londonderry or Tyrone, application may be made to either address.

The website for the Probate and Matrimonial Office in Belfast is www.courtsni.gov.uk. The Royal Courts of Justice is also at www.courtsni.gov.uk. To contact the Londonderry District Probate Registry, telephone 028 7126 1832.

Fees due for probate applications

• Net estate under £10,000:	nil
• Net estate of £10,000 and upwards:	£200

• If the deceased resided elsewhere in Northern Ireland, the application must be made to the Belfast office (for contact details, see box, below).

The fees in all applications are based on the net value of the estate (see box, above). For an estate over £10,000 the fee is £250 on a personal application. Personal applications must be made in person – that is, not by post. The fees increase from time to time with little prior warning, so it is best to check with the appropriate Probate Office before writing the cheque.

> **❝It is not necessary to serve a notice on an executor who is not acting and who has not renounced. ❞**

Inheritance Tax (IHT) payments

The cheque for IHT due should be made out to 'HM Revenue & Customs' and the cheque for the Probate Office fees should be made out to 'Northern Ireland Court Service'.

Form PA1

In Northern Ireland, it is not necessary to serve a notice on an executor who is not acting and who has not renounced. It is therefore possible for one executor to obtain probate, without another even being aware he or she is an executor.

Transfer of a property

While property is registered or unregistered as in England and Wales, land law legislation generally in Northern Ireland is very different from that in England and Wales.

In the case of registered land, the executors or administrators complete assent **form 17**. The completed form 17 is then sent to the Land Registers of Northern Ireland in Belfast at the Land

 At this stage, the internet service for the Land Registers of Northern Ireland (LRNI) is only available to members of the public at the LRNI public counters at Lincoln Building, 27-45 Great Victoria Street, Belfast BT2 7SL.

and Property Services (see page 193),
together with the land certificate, the
original grant of probate or letters of
administration and **form 100A**
(Application for Registration).

- Both forms are available from the Land
  Registers (see box, below opposite).
- The fee is £75.

If the property is subject to a
mortgage, the certificate of charge with
the 'vacate' or receipt sealed by the bank
or building society should be lodged at
the same time.

Unregistered land is, in fact, registered
in the Registry of Deeds, held at the
Land Registers. Although no particular
form of words is required in order to vest
property in a beneficiary, the wording
varies both as to whether the title to the
property is freehold, 'fee farm grant', or
leasehold. In these cases, ask a solicitor
to prepare an assent for unregistered
land. The solicitor can arrange for a
memorial of the assent to be registered
in the Registry of Deeds, for which the
Registry charges a fee of £13. The
memorial is an extract of the assent
giving the date, names of the parties
executing the deed, the address of the
property and whether the property is
freehold or leasehold.

**❝ If a property is subject
to a mortgage, the
certificate of charge
should be lodged with
forms 17 and 100A.❞**

Entitlement on intestacy

The main difference between English and Northern Ireland law about wills and probate relates to the rules on intestacy. In Northern Ireland, unlike in England and Wales, no life interests are created on intestacy.

As in England, the nearest relatives in a fixed order are entitled to apply for the grant of letter of administration (see page 11) and, if the nearest relative does not wish to be an administrator, he or she can renounce the right to do so, in favour of the next nearest relative.

 Administering an intestate estate can be dangerous territory, as the rules are so very specific. It is best to always consult a solicitor.

DECEASED LEAVES SURVIVING SPOUSE OR CIVIL PARTNER ...

The surviving spouse or civil partner normally becomes the administrator. Where there is a surviving spouse or civil partner, he or she is always entitled to the deceased's personal effects, no matter how great their value.

... and children

If there are two or more children, the surviving spouse or civil partner only receives £250,000 and one-third of the residue, with two-thirds divided between the remaining children. This rule applies no matter how many children there are. If there is only one child, the surviving spouse or civil partner receives £250,000 and one-half of the residue and the child receives the other half of the residue.

... with no children but parents

Where someone dies intestate without children but with one or both parents still alive, the surviving spouse or civil

> **❝** A surviving spouse or civil partner is entitled to the deceased's personal effects, no matter how great their value. **❞**

partner receives the first £450,000 of the estate together with half the residue. The other half of the residue passes to the parents of the intestate equally or, if only one parent is still alive, to that parent in its entirety.

... with no children or parents, but brothers and sisters

Where someone dies without children and parents but with brothers or sisters or children of predeceased brothers and sisters, the surviving spouse or civil partner takes the first £450,000 of the estate together with half of the residue. The other half of the residue is divided between the surviving brothers and sisters. The children of a predeceased brother or sister divide their parent's share equally between them.

DECEASED LEAVES NO SURVIVING SPOUSE OR CIVIL PARTNER ...

If there is no surviving spouse or civil partner, the entire estate is divided equally between the children. If any child has died before the intestate, the children of the deceased child divide their parent's share between them. As in England, no distinction is made between natural or adopted children.

... and no children but parents

The parents inherit the entire estate equally or, if only one parent survives, that parent inherits the entire estate.

... and no children or parents, but brothers and sisters

In these circumstances, the entire estate is divided between the brothers and sisters, with the issue of any predeceased brother or sister taking their parent's share.

❝ If there is no surviving spouse or civil partner, the entire estate is divided equally between the children. ❞

 In Northern Ireland, in the case of there being no spouse or civil partner, issue, parents, siblings, grandparents or uncles or aunts or their issue, there is a special order of precedence to determine the next of kin. Consult a solicitor.

Glossary

Lay executors need to understand clearly the meaning of legal terminology and expressions used in connection with wills and probate. Some of them are obscure or unusual. Always check if you are uncertain. The most commonly used words and expressions are listed below.

Administrator: The name given to a personal representative if not appointed by a valid will. The administrator will usually have to obtain letters of administration to show that he or she is the person with legal authority to deal with the property of the deceased.

Affidavit: A declaration in writing made upon oath before someone who is authorised to administer oaths.

Assets: The value of an estate.

Beneficiary: A person (or persons) who benefits from a will

Bequest: A gift of a particular object or cash (as opposed to 'devise', which means land or buildings).

Chattels: Personal belongings: for example, jewellery, furniture, wine, pictures, books, even cars and horses not used for business. Does not include money or investments.

Child (referred to in a will or intestacy): Child of the deceased including adopted and illegitimate children but, unless specifically included in a will, not stepchildren.

Class of persons: A group of people with a particular common link, e.g. all my grandchildren, or all my first cousins.

Codicil: A document that alters an existing will.

Co-habitee: A partner of the deceased who may be able to claim a share of the estate. The term 'common law wife' has no legal force.

Confirmation: The Scottish term used to describe both the English terms 'probate' and 'letters of administration'.

Contingent: Where an event must happen before a gift can be made, e.g. the beneficiary must reach 21 before any payment can be made. The 18-year-old therefore has a contingent rather than an absolute entitlement to the money.

Crown: The government of a constitutional monarchy.

Demise: A grant of a lease.

Devise: A gift of house or land.

Disposition: A formal conveyancing document in Scotland.

Domicile: The country you consider to be your permanent home even if you actually reside elsewhere. It is distinct from nationality and place of residence.

Enduring Power of Attorney: A form that authorises someone to act on another's behalf. It is no longer possible to create new ones.

Estate: All the assets and property of the deceased, including houses, cars, investments, money and personal belongings.

Excepted estate: One that is less than £325,000 or more than £325,000 but less than £1,000,000 and no IHT is payable because the estate passes to a spouse or a charity.

Executor: The name given to a personal representative if appointed by a valid will or codicil. The executor will usually have to apply for probate of the will to show that he or she is the person with legal authority to deal with the property of the deceased.

Executor-dative: In Scotland, an administrator appointed by the court for a person who dies intestate.

Executor-nominate: The Scottish term for the English term 'executor'.

Grant of probate: The document issued by the probate registry to the executors of a will to authorise them to administer the estate.

Guardian: A person who would become responsible for your children in the event of your death before your children are 18 years old.

Heritable estate: Land and buildings in Scotland.

Inheritance Tax (IHT): The tax that may be payable when the total estate of the deceased person exceeds a set threshold (subject to various exemptions and adjustments).

Intestate: A person who dies without making a will.

Issue: Your children and all generations arising from them – grandchildren, great-grandchildren, and so on.

Lasting Power of Attorney: Supercedes Enduring Power of Attorney (see above).

Legacy: A gift of money or object.

Letters of administration: The document issued by the probate registry to the administrator of the estate of an intestate person.

Letters of administration with will annexed: The document issued by the probate registry to the administrator when there is a will but the will does not deal with everything, e.g. it fails to appoint an executor.

Life interest: A gift that gives someone the right to income from an asset or the right to occupation of a property for the duration of their life after which the asset or property passes to someone else mentioned in the gift (known as the remainderman).

Life tenant: The person who enjoys the benefit for life.

Minor: A person under 18 years of age.

Moveable estate: Property other than land and buildings in Scotland.

Named person: A person who is named in the will.

Next of kin: The person entitled to the estate when a person dies intestate.

Personal estate or personalty: All the investments and belongings of a person apart from land and buildings.

Personal representative: A general term for both administrators and executors.

Prior rights: In Scotland, rights to the house, its furnishings and a cash sum. Except in the case of larger estates, where intestacy is rare, prior rights often mean that the surviving spouse inherits the entire estate. The financial figures given here are reviewed from time to time and as at 2009 have not been changed since 2005.

Probate of the will: The document issued to executors by a probate registry in England, Wales and Northern Ireland to authorise them to administer the estate.

Probate Registry: The government office that deals with probate matters. The Principal Probate Registry is in London with district registries in cities and some large towns.

Real estate or realty: Land and buildings owned by a person.

Remaindermen: The persons who get an asset on the death of the life tenant.

Residuary beneficiary: A person who gets or shares what is left of the estate after all debts, taxes and specific legacies have been paid.

Residue: What is left of the estate to share out after all the debts and specific bequests and legacies have been paid.

Solvent: Value of the assets exceeds any debts and liabilities.

Specific bequests: Particular items gifted by will. They may be referred to as 'specific legacies'.

Testator: A person who makes a will.

Trustee: A person responsible for administering a trust.

Will: The document in which you say what is to happen to your possessions on your death.

Useful addresses

England and Wales

Age Concern England
Astral House
1268 London Road
London SW16 4ER
Tel: 0800 009966
www.ageconcern.org.uk

FT Interactive Data
Fitzroy House
Epworth Street
London EC2A 4DL
Tel: 020 7825 8000
www.ftid.com
(For back copies of the Stock Exchange
Daily Official List)

General Register Office
PO Box 2
Southport, Merseyside
PR8 2JD
Tel: 0845 603 7788
www.gro.gov.uk

HM Courts Service
(for information on probate and
further addresses)
Customer Service Unit
5th Floor
Clive House
Petty France
London SW1H 9HD
Tel: 020 7189 2000
www.hmcourts-service.gov.uk/cms/wills

**HM Revenue & Customs Capital
Taxes**
Ferrers House
PO Box 38
Castle Meadow Road
Nottingham NG2 1BB
Tel: 0845 302 0900 (Inheritance Tax
helpline and probate)
www.hmrc.gov.uk
www.hmrc.gov.uk/inheritancetax

Institute of Professional Will Writers
Trinity Point
New Road
Halesowen
West Midlands B63 3HY
Tel: 08456 442042
www.ipw.org.uk

International Pension Centre
Tyneview Park
Newcastle-upon-Tyne
NE98 1BE
Tel: 0191 218 7777
www.thepensionservice.gov.uk

Land Registry
32 Lincoln's Inn Fields
London WC2A 3PH
Tel: 020 7917 8888
www.landregistry.gov.uk
(Use the website to find your local area
offices)

The Law Society
The Law Society's Hall
113 Chancery Lane
London WC2A 1PL
www.lawsociety.org.uk
(For information on solicitors specialising in
wills and probate)

London Gazette
PO Box 7923
London SE1 5ZH
Tel: 020 7394 4517
www.gazettes-online.co.uk

National Savings & Investments (NS&I)
Glasgow G58 1SB
Enquiries about Cash ISAs, Investment
Accounts, Capital Bonds, Ordinary Accounts

Blackpool FY3 9YP
Enquiries about Premium Bonds, Income
Bonds, Pensioners' Guaranteed Bonds,
Guaranteed Equity Bonds

Tel: 0845 964 5000
(Central helpline for enquiries about
NS&I products, including advice on filling
in form NSA 904 'Death of a Holder of
National Savings')
www.nsandi.com

Office of the Public Guardianship
Customer Services
PO Box 15118
Birmingham B16 6GX
Tel: 0845 330 2900
www.guardianship.gov.uk

Oyez Straker
Tel: 0800 483 434
info@oyezstarker.co.uk
www.oyezformslink.co.uk
(Telesales for probate forms and other
stationery)

The Pension Service
Tyneview Park
Whitley Road
Newcastle upon Tyne
NE98 1BA
Tel: 0845 606 0265
www.dwp.gov.uk
www.thepensionservice.gov.uk

Principal Probate Registry
First Avenue House
42–49 High Holborn
London WC1V 6NP
Tel: 020 7947 6939
Helpline: 0845 302 0900 (for IHT
and probate information, and for
probate packs)
www.hmcourts-service.gov.uk

**Principal Registry of the Family
Division**
see Principal Probate Registry

Royal Courts of Justice
Strand
London WC2A 2LL
Tel: 020 7947 6000
www.hmcourts-service.gov.uk

Society of Trust and Estate Practitioners (STEP)
Artillery House
11–19 Artillery Row
London SW1P 1RT
Tel: 020 7340 0500
www.step.org

Society of Will Writers
Eagle House
Exchange Road
Lincoln LN6 3JZ
Tel: 01522 687888
www.thesocietyofwillwriters.co.uk

Scotland

Accountant of Court
Child Unit
Office of the Public Guardian
Hadrian House
Callendar Business Park
Falkirk FK1 1XR
Tel: 01324 678300
www.scotcourts.gov.uk

Edinburgh Gazette
TSO Scotland
26 Rutland Square
Edinburgh EH1 2BW
Tel: 0131 659 7032
www.edinburgh-gazette.co.uk

General Register Office for Scotland
New Register House
3 West Register Street
Edinburgh EH1 3YT
Tel: 0131 334 0380
www.gro-scotland.gov.uk

HM Revenue & Customs Capital Taxes (Scotland)
Meldrum House
15 Drumsheugh Gardens
Edinburgh EH3 7UG
Tel: 0131 777 4293
www.hmrc.gov.uk
www.hmrc.gov.uk/inheritancetax

Law Society of Scotland
26 Drumsheugh Gardens
Edinburgh EH3 7YR
Tel: 0131 226 7411
www.lawscot.org.uk
lawscot@lawscot.org.uk

Registers of Scotland
Customer Service Centre
Erskine House
68 Queen Street
Edinburgh EH2 4NF
Tel: 0845 607 0161
OR
Customer Service Centre
9 George Square
Glasgow G2 1DY
Tel: 0845 6070164
www.ros.gov.uk

Sheriff Clerks' Office
Commissary Department
27 Chambers Street
Edinburgh EH1 1LB
Tel: 0131 247 2806
www.scotcourts.gov.uk

Northern Ireland

Age Concern Northern Ireland
3 Lower Crescent
Belfast, BT7 1NR
Tel: 028 9024 5729
www.ageconcernni.org

Belfast Gazette
The Stationery Office
16 Arthur Street
Belfast BT1 4GD
Tel: 028 9089 5135
www.gazettes-online.co.uk
Belfast.gazette.comments@tso.co.uk

District Probate Registry
The Court House
Bishop Street
Londonderry BT48 7PY
Tel: 028 7126 1832
for people living in Londonderry (Derry),
Fermanagh and Tyrone
(For free booklet, *Step-by-step guide to
personal probate applications*)

**HM Revenue & Customs Capital Taxes
(Northern Ireland)**
Level 3 Dorchester House
52–58 Great Victoria Street
Belfast BT2 7QL
Tel: 028 9050 5353
www.hmrc.gov.uk
www.hmrc.gov.uk/inheritancetax

Land and Property Services
Lincoln Building
27–45 Great Victoria Street
Belfast BT2 7SL
Tel: 028 9025 1515
www.lrni.gov.uk

Law Society of Northern Ireland
40 Linenhall Street
Belfast BT2 8BA
Tel: 028 9023 1614
www.lawsoc-ni.org
info@lawsoc-ni.org

Probate Office
Royal Courts of Justice
Chichester Street
Belfast BT1 3JF
Tel: 028 9032 8594
www.courtsni.gov.uk

Public Record Office of Northern Ireland
66 Balmoral Avenue
Belfast BT9 6NY
Tel: 028 9025 5905
www.proni.nics.gov.uk
proni@dcalni.gov.uk

Index

Index

which?

Which? is the leading independent consumer champion in the UK. A not-for-profit organisation, we exist to make individuals as powerful as the organisations they deal with in everyday life. The next few pages give you a taster of our many products and services. For more information, log onto www.which.co.uk or call 0800 252 100.

Which? magazine

Which? magazine has a simple goal in life – to offer truly independent advice to consumers that they can genuinely trust – from which credit card to use through to which washing machine to buy. Every month the magazine is packed with 84 advertisement-free pages of expert advice on the latest products. It takes on the biggest of businesses on behalf of all consumers and is not afraid to tell consumers to avoid their products. Truly the consumer champion. To subscribe, go to www.which.co.uk.

Which? online

www.which.co.uk gives you access to all Which? content online and much, much more. It's updated regularly, so you can read hundreds of product reports and Best Buy recommendations, keep up to date with Which? campaigns, compare products, use our financial planning tools and search for the best cars on the market. You can also access reviews from *The Good Food Guide*, register for email updates and browse our online shop – so what are you waiting for? To subscribe, go to www.which.co.uk.

Which? Legal Service

Which? Legal Service offers immediate access to first-class legal advice from qualified lawyers at unrivalled value. One low-cost annual subscription allows members to enjoy unlimited legal advice by telephone on a wide variety of legal topics, including consumer law – problems with goods and services, employment law, holiday problems, neighbour disputes, parking tickets, clamping fines and tenancy advice for private residential tenants in England and Wales. To subscribe, call 01992 822 828 or go to www.whichlegalservice.co.uk.

Which? Local

Using a trader can be a bit hit and miss. But using one who's been recommended can help ensure a more reliable service. Which? Local is an easy to use website with thousands of recommendations for local traders across the UK reviewed by Which? members. From plumbers to builders, tree surgeons to hairdressers, Which? Local's listings have saved members time and money. If you're already a Which? member or want to find out more, visit www.which-local.co.uk. To find out how you can become a member call 01992 822 800.

Which? Computing

If you own a computer, are thinking of buying one or just want to keep abreast of the latest technology and keep up with your kids, there's one invaluable source of information you can turn to – *Which? Computing* magazine. *Which? Computing* offers you honest, unbiased reviews of new technology, problem-solving tips from the experts and step-by-step guides to help you make the most of your computer. To subscribe, go to www.which.co.uk.

Which? Money

Whether you want to boost your pension, make your savings work harder or simply need to find the best credit card, *Which? Money* has the information you need. *Which? Money* offers you honest, unbiased reviews of the best (and worst) new personal finance deals, from bank accounts to loans, credit cards to savings accounts. Throughout the magazine you will find tips and ideas to make your budget go further plus dozens of Best Buys. To subscribe, go to www.which.co.uk.

which?

Which? Books

Which? Books provide impartial, expert advice on everyday matters from finance to law, property and major life events. We also publish the country's most trusted restaurant guide, *The Good Food Guide*. To find out more about Which? Books, log on to www.which.co.uk or call 01903 828557.

Other books in this series

NEW EDITION

The Tax Handbook 2009/10

Tony Levene
ISBN: 978 1 84490 060 2
Price £10.99

Make sense of the complicated rules, legislation and red tape with *Tax Handbook 2009/10*. Written by the *Guardian* personal finance journalist and award-winning consumer champion Tony Levene, this guide gives expert advice on all aspects of the UK tax system and does the legwork for you. It includes information on finding the right accountant and how to get the best from them, NI contributions, VAT and tax credits for families. This new edition also contains updates from the 2009 Budget, disability credits, tax advice on cars, the latest news on the Taxpayers' Charter and step-by-step advice on completing the self-assessment form.

Giving and Inheriting

Jonquil Lowe
ISBN: 978 1 84490 032 9
Price £10.99

Inheritance Tax (IHT) is becoming a major worry for more and more people. *Giving and Inheriting* is an essential guide to estate planning and tax liability, offering advice from an acknowledged financial expert. This book also features information on equity release, trusts and lifetime gifts.

Which? Books

which?

Which? Books

Other books in this series

Care Options in Retirement
Margaret Wallace and Philip Spiers
ISBN: 978 1 84490 053 4
Price £10.99

Here is the definitive guide to the financial and legal considerations of care for older people. The book provides information on the types of housing and care available, from care at home and retirement housing to respite care and care homes. Differences in Scotland, Wales and Northern Ireland are highlighted as well as special considerations for meeting specific religious and mental health needs. Whether you need to know about benefits, support services, renting or buying retirement housing or want advice on how to interpret a care home's inspection report, you will find useful tips and information.

Money Saving Handbook
Tony Levene
ISBN: 978 1 84490 048 0
Price £10.99

From low-cost air travel and zero per cent finance to cheap mobile phone tariffs, the list of financial products is endless and the good deals are harder to find. Personal finance expert Tony Levene separates the cons from the bargains and explains how to avoid hidden charges and penalty fees. *Money Saving Handbook* is the key to becoming smarter with your money.

Buy, Sell and Move House
Kate Faulkner
ISBN: 978 1 84490 056 5
Price £10.99

This new edition of the Which? best-selling property guide covers the latest changes to HIPs and analysis of the property market. From dealing with estate agents to chasing solicitors and working out the true cost of your move, this guide tells you how to keep things on track and avoid painful sticking points.

Making your will online with Which? involves completing a simple but comprehensive online questionnaire that tailors your will to your particular circumstances. The service is supported by a telephone advice line where specialist solicitors will be on hand to answer any questions throughout the process. Once your questionnaire has been completed, it will automatically be sent to a solicitor to be checked, and then it will be ready for you to download and print it.

Reasons to make your will online with Which?

- Gain peace of mind
- Appoint guardians and make provisions for children
- Plan the distribution of your estate
- Prevent family disputes
- Leave instructions about your funeral or cremation
- Fully supported by specialist solicitors

How much will my will cost me using my exclusive discount?

£79 for a single will (normal price £89)

£119 for a 'mirror will' (individual wills for you and your partner, normal price £129)

To obtain your discount, start writing your will at www.whichwills.com and use the voucher code WH-WANDP at payment stage.

Closing date of discounted offer: 30 June 2011.

Please note:

Which? Will writing service is an online service only.

The service is not compatible with law in Scotland.

We do not provide storage of your will.

For enquiries about the Which? Will writing package, telephone 02380 857486.